"Now it is time for Black men to put guns down and pick up the real amour of your Devine purpose for which you have been created by your Father who is in heaven: Reclaim the position as leader. Protect and subdue the earth for God's Glory.

— *the Author*

We the People

insure domestic Tranquility, provide for the common *...*
and our Posterity, do ordain and establish this Consti*...*

Article I

UNCLE
SAM MAKES A POOR
BABY DADDY

A story of female head of household communties

JANE TALLEY

Printed in the United States of America

First Printing, January 2019

ISBN: 978-1729346426

Bold Venture Press
Sunrise, FL

www.boldventurepress.com

Contents

Dedication

This Book is divinely inspired by the Creator to bring His sons back into alignment within His Purpose.

This book is dedicated to the millions of broken families who came through public assistance programs over the past fifty years.

And to my father Joseph Crittenden, who modeled the perfect father and family head, inspiring me to want every child to experience the benefits of this kind of fatherhood. And to my husband who has been a wonderful father to our children.

Vital to the pursuit of Happiness.

Introduction

True, there is a segment of our population who are privileged. It is a natural fact those on top would be reluctant to give up or share such prestige or status. When I taught life classes at Boaz and Ruth's (a restoration program, located in the heart of the ghetto, serving predominantly black males coming out of prison), I asked a question. I asked the men if they would be willing to give up or share top positions of prestige if they had it. They all answered no. My objective for asking the question was to have them to see the other side.

My aim in this book is not to ask those at the top to voluntarily share their position. What I am aiming for, is to move a population from a victim position to one of empowerment without violence or taking on old unfair practices and/or exploitation to get there.

My goal is to excite the underdog to see their potential to rise to their place of prestige and power with a sense of service and leadership without old ways of exploitation engrained in America's capitalistic mantra. Now the fight for fair, equal right and entitlements have come a long way, while not far enough, to use those existing advances to propel them to be the head not the tail ... to move them to a new spiritual advance order. Let this be the time to be proactive and not so much reactive.

Let's Go!

In the Beginning

In the midst of today's violence, we search for answers. We raise the question, "Why are folks so angry?" There are perhaps as many answers as there are violent acts. The common thread through each act of violence is the perpetrator's search for justice to right the perceived wrong made against him or her. Granted, the perpetrators do not always understand exactly why they feel wronged. However, elements of chaos are reflective in each act of violence, whether it is in their thought processes, values, or structural disorganization. In any case, the perpetrators are motivated to seek revenge as they act out their aggressions.

In many cases, answers to unexplained mysteries of human behavior can be found in the primitive behaviors of the wild animal kingdom … as in the case of the unexplained killings of hundreds rhinoceroses in South African's wild game reserve, Pilanesberg.

Can the animal kingdom teach us a lesson? I believe it can.

"The Delinquents, A Spate of Rhino Killings" was a story first reported by the late Bob Simon in 1999 on the CBS program *60 Minutes*. Game rangers discovered an unusual numbers of dead white rhinos in the South African bush, which rangers had spent years protecting.

South Africa's Pilanesberg Wildlife Reserve had suffered the slaughter of 10 percent of the once-thriving population of rhinos in the park. The rhinos' horns hadn't been touched signaling the killings weren't the work of poachers. An investigation revealed the prime suspects were actually young male orphan elephants who had grown up without role models.

"I think everyone needs a role model, and these elephants had no role model and no idea of what appropriate elephant behavior was," said Gus van Dyk, Pilanesberg Park's field ecologist.

More than twenty years earlier, the Kruger National Park had too many elephants. Kruger was South Africa's largest conservation area. With no way to relocate the large adult elephants, researchers decided to kill the adults and transport their young to other parks. Governmental officials considered the young elephants might not adjust well, but felt they had no other options.

One of the suspects in the rhino killings was an elephant named Tom Thumb who was seen in an area where a rhino was killed. Tom Thumb was put under surveillance. Other elephants were caught red handed. In addition to killing rhinos, the young elephants were acting aggressively toward tourist vehicles. Having no alternative, researchers eventually decided to kill five of the elephants. Tom Thumb was among those spared.

So, about humans …

Evangelist Daniel Kolenda of Christ for All Nations reminds us a mother abandoning a child at birth is a crime. "A mother's job is not done when she gives birth to a child. With birth, 'motherhood' and 'nurturing' takes on a much more important dimension. It is also in the Kingdom Of God."

But preaching doesn't seem to reach all those who need to hear those words.

But a further, and much bigger problem, is the thousands of babies abandoned daily by fathers.

Yet, a man leaving his baby behind is not considered a crime.

Abandonment by fathers has never been designated as a civil crime, but surely the misdeed is immoral and a sin in the eyes of God. The father's presence or lack of presence in the family has the most dramatic influence on the socialization of his children. Like the elephants, these babies are growing up like orphans without role models.

If society is to change for the better, today's critical epidemic of fatherless "families" must command attention. Putting "father" back in the family is probably the most noble and worthy cause deserving attention, time and resources today.

Children are being deprived of the proven positive benefits of a married two-parent household. The quality of life among children growing up outside of two-parent households is seriously diminished. The family is the seat of a child's socialization, where lessons on moral character, civility, empathy and love are taught. Broken families without male role models as moral compasses are leading youth to kill each other over trivial things such as a pair of tennis shoes, a piece of birthday cake or feeling they have been disrespected.

The fatherless children of today's human society are no different than the young male elephants that had grown up without role models. In both instances the onset of violence resulted from the disruption of their social order. Human children being abandoned by fathers, an epidemic phenomenon, has brought on today's violence.

The children didn't become fatherless simply because men ran away or abandoned the traditional family.

The situation evolved from targeted discriminatory public welfare legislation and the systemic gender-specific racial discrimination attached to the welfare system.

Working in tandem, the actions of these two elements — discriminatory welfare and gender-specific racial discrimination — discouraged fathers from being involved in taking care of their families.

Instead of cementing the family, the system drove fathers out and set up a situation where they were not financially able to participate with the family. Over the past five decades, these schemes have resulted in the successful dismantling of intact families and the destruction of the black male's sense of purpose.

Constitutional rights of children have been infringed upon. Children have been denied living conditions vital to achieving their constitutional rights of life, liberty and the pursuit of happiness. Conditions vital to these constitutional guarantees, which have been either destroyed or purposefully neglected, must somehow now be restored.

"The family" is the most profound institution necessary for the development of our humanity and civility. Families are the primary socializing agents for children and the foundation of human society.

Some governmental programs have attempted to promote fatherhood improvement, but there is no statistical evidence two parent households have increased as a result. The blur of years allowing children to remain fatherless has clearly put the traditional family in crisis.

The statistical evidence of the negative results of broken families does include higher crime rates, higher suicide rates, and higher rates of drug abuse, to name just a few.

A list of benefits and advantages to children growing up with married parents was compiled by family scholars from U. C. Berkeley, Rutgers University, Universities of Texas, Virginia, Minnesota, Chicago, Maryland and Washington DC in 2015, published as "Why Marriage Matters (third edition): Thirty Conclusions from the Social Sciences. The report concludes the children in whole marriages live longer, healthier lives both physically and psychologically. The report shows those children:

- Do better in school.
- Are more likely to graduate high school and attend college.
- Are less likely to live in poverty.
- Are less likely to be in trouble with the law.
- Are less likely to drink or do drugs.
- Are less likely to be violent or sexually active.
- Are less likely to be victims of sexual or physical violence.
- Are more likely to have a successful marriage.

Many studies recognized a father's absence is associated with a host of social problems, including an increased probability of family poverty and heightened risk of delinquency.

At my church each year on Father's Day, one person is selected to be "Father of the Year."

This year, the chosen father told the congregation about his difficulties in life living without knowing his own father and how he overcame those difficulties with the aid of a loving relative.

Later I talked with him in more depth.

Sam, not his real name of course, shared how other kids teased him about not having a father. He said the taunts made him feel unloved. In spite of his loving mother who raised him in the projects in the South, he felt left out because everyone else had a father.

Every summer, Sam's mother sent him to his Grandpa Edgar's tobacco farm to get him off the street and to teach him responsibility. Sam had not gotten into any serious trouble but said he carried a chip on his shoulder and was prone to get into scrapes. Sam was academically astute as an honor student and athlete, yet he admitted he was not very popular in school.

Sam told me his "Grandpa" was actually his grandmother's brother, but he called him Grandpa because all the other kids called him that. He recalled how he appreciated the way "Grandpa" talked to him and guided him into making good decisions. Sam said Grandpa taught him reasoning with home-spun logic. Sam acknowledged learning about marriage through observation of "Grandpa's" relationship with his wife and family. The experience fashioned his image of what a family should be.

On one of those summer days, at a time when the South was still segregated and Sam was a tall teenager, he accompanied his Grandpa with other black men to a nearby white-owned farm. At the end of the job, the workers lined up to receive their pay. His Grandpa checked with Sam to see what he had been paid. The foreman had short changed Sam, as a child. Sam said Grandpa went to the foreman and told him his nephew Sam had done a man's day's work and deserved a man's wages. Sam expressed how proud he felt to have been referenced as doing a man's day's work and described it as a rite of passage.

Sam's Grandpa became a role model for him and interrupted what could have been the wrong path. Not only did he show Sam how to be a man but demonstrated how to be a husband and a father.

At church, when Sam was recognized as Father of the Year, he had completed a college education, married, had children of his own. He is a top psychiatrist in private practice and at a hospital.

For some time studies recognized "fathers absence" is associated with a host of social problems including an increased probability of family poverty and heightened risk of delinquency. The three most prominent effects according to a 1990 report from the Department of Justice are lower intellectual development, higher levels of illegitimate teenage parenting, and higher levels of welfare dependency. According to the report, more often than not, missing and "throwaway" children come from single-parent families, families with step parents, and cohabiting-adult families. This information comes from The Real Root Causes of Violent Crime: The Breakdown of Marriage, Family, and Community by Patrick F. Fagan, Ph.D.

Despite the earlier recognition of a source of the social structure's decline, the presence of intact families with mothers, fathers, and children are perpetually moving in the wrong direction — toward extinction. Nationally, the worst case scenario has been the Black family where less than 30% of the children are born to intact families. Because African-American are the least likely to be married among all races in this country, Black children are least likely to benefit from socialization by both parents. Black men by the millions have abandoned their children, leaving them to be taken care of by mothers and Uncle Sam.

This phenomenon is not occurring due to some genetic abnormality or inferiority among Black men, but because of intentional betrayals by Uncle Sam, leaving mothers broken and hopeless. A shameful seventy two percent (72%) of African-American babies born in our Nation in 2016 were born to unwed mothers. These broken and abandoned women settled into a state of complacency and depression believing it is just the way life is and there's nothing they can do about it. These women have to be taught now to believe — like the old rendition of Sam Cooke's song — "A Change is Gonna Come."

There is work ahead.

My hypothesis: The solution to this family crisis is to bring men into their families as responsible heads of household — not just as outside fathers participating from the sidelines — but they must be inside and intact as married husbands, fathers, and heads of the household.

Most believe that all lives matter and that Black lives surely matter. Lives matter not only when confronted by the police but when conception occurs and when babies are born. Blacks' lives, like all lives are of value from conception to the grave. Too many black men see pregnancy as a "situation" rather than a potential "person." The lives of these babies are of equal value to all lives and must be treated as such. The babies must be nurtured, loved and cared by both parents as a valued commodity from the instant of conception. When men run from their pregnant girlfriends or sex partners, they are throwing away their own flesh and blood and are not seeing that Black lives matter

When men abandon one baby and go on to conceive another baby and then abandon the second one too, the babies are throwaways … orphans.

Agencies, protest groups, structured government assistance programs, have serious political agendas targeting abortion clinics and Planned Parenthood under the disguise of fighting for the rights of the unborn children being thrown away by means of medical procedures. What about the blatant disregard for the babies born into low income families where fathers throw away their own flesh and blood by means of abandonment? Don't those Black lives matter? Do the lives of the fathers, the mothers, and the throwaway children matter? *You bet they do!*

All these lives should matter, long before confrontations with police in demonstrations demanding we value Black lives. Serious discrimination and mal-treatment by police or any entity is not to be tolerated. But, if we want to reduce circumstances requiring police involvement at all, we must return fathers to their rightful place, as the moral compass for the family.

Humans are driven, to a great extent, by a sense of self-worth. Self-worth starts in the cradle. Whether parents are present or not they are the first teachers and reflection of their children's sense of self-worth. Whether a parent is present or absent, children still define self-worth by their progenitors. When parents are absent, the child still asks: Why did my parent leave me? Was I not good enough?

Love of self is created in an environment of love, especially within the context of an intact family.

The value of self-worth must be taught to have priority over material value. This scale is often confused in low wealth communities. Trappings of material wealth provide an illusion of self-worth. For example, a teen and mother may feel the latest style or name brand jacket must be worn so the teen feels self-worth. The mother may skip paying her rent in order to buy this jacket so, from her view, the teen will be perceived as worthy. Because these high price commodities are seen as establishing self-worth, they are often the targets of thefts, fights and even murders. Individuals in poverty want to appear as if they have money therefore defining themselves as worthy. For poor people, material trappings such as gold chains, fancy cars, expensive tennis shoes, and brand name sportswear items take on a desperate attempt to help individuals be compared to those having real financial wealth.

PERSPECTIVE
My World

I grew up with one older sister, along with my mother and father in the Randolph Neighborhood within the "real" West End of Richmond Virginia. I specifically say it was the "real" West End because the Western part of Henrico today is all too often referred to as" The West End" making no distinction from the west end of Henrico County and West End of the City of Richmond. My home was located on Lombardy Street between Parkwood Avenue and West Cary Street. A large portion of the West End was destroyed for the construction of the Powhite Parkway and the RMA Lombardy toll plaza stands where my house once stood. Randolph was one of many tight-knit Black communities in Richmond.

Richmond, Virginia, was the Capital of the Confederacy. I grew up during the 1950s, when Blacks were called Negroes or Colored people. We lived completely in all Black communities. Our schools, churches and businesses were all segregated.

In those days, there were no school buses and we walked to school regardless of weather. We attended segregated neighborhood schools and often passed white schools to get to our Black-only school. If we had to walk through a white neighborhood, white folks sitting on the porches would call out ugly racial slurs as we passed. We learned to look straight ahead as if we did not hear them but our hearts were pounding with fear and anger.

I attended the Randolph Elementary school which housed grades from kindergarten to the seventh grade. Benjamin A. Graves Junior High School was the only other middle/Junior High school in Richmond for all Black children in the 7th & 8th grades. Armstrong High School and Maggie L. Walker High School were the only two black high schools in Richmond. Most West End residents, including me, attended Maggie L. Walker High School. I graduated in 1962.

The two high schools were known for their annual football rivalry played every year on Thanksgiving Weekend. It was a major event for the city attracting more than 20,000 attendees. Everyone wore the colors of their favorite school —either green and white or orange and blue. Blacks throughout the city decorated their homes, cars and businesses in school colors.

We were poor according to majority standards. In the West End of the city everyone knew everyone intimately and looked out for each other's homes and children. Neighbors had as much right to correct a child as did a parent. It was a matter of trusting each other because we had the same unified hopes and dreams for our families. "Home-Training" as discipline was referred to, was a major element of the family. Children were taught misbehavior outside the home, at school, or in the community, brought a poor reflection on family. A child who was punished at school for misbehaving, also received additional punishment at home. Parents would say: "You can't go around acting like you got no home training."

The community in Richmond in the 1950s was thoroughly segregated as a legacy of the Virginia Public Assemblages Act of 1926, which required the "separation of white and colored persons at public halls, theaters, opera houses, motion picture shows, and places of public entertainment and public assemblages." (*Segregation, Massive Resistance, and Deseg-*

regation: Personal Reflections on Growing up in Richmond, Virginia — 1950-1967, by Kenneth E. Whitlock, Jr. 1/21/13)

But we lived in mixed income neighborhoods. My block had a school teacher, Arthur Godfrey's chauffeur, a famous radio and TV host, a shoe repairman, a tailor, domestic workers, a minister and a nurse. Although sharing among families was common, we had one very poor family every other family helped by sharing food and clothing. My aunt often bathed some of the children.

Men in my neighborhood generally worked outside of the home and the women added to the income by working in white folks' homes doing laundry, cleaning houses and cooking.

Some in the neighborhood, like my father's sister, had college degrees. She was a school teacher.

My father was a tailor and worked at the prestigious Newman's Men's Clothing Store in the heart of downtown. In later years, my mother worked at the same store as a seamstress. Life from my perspective was almost perfect. The milk man, the ice man, and the vegetable man with horse drawn buggies were common sights on my street. Our generation was isolated, nurtured and sheltered from racial issues with few exceptions.

My childhood was peaceful. During the morning hours of the summer, we played "outside" games dressed in our morning clothes (older shorts and tops). We played such games as jack rocks, card games, hop scotch, rock school and marbles. These games did not cause us to exert ourselves in the heat of the morning. There was no air conditioning in the average homes. During the afternoon everyone went home to take a bath and "dress for the evening," as we called it. Evening clothes were nicer than our morning clothes ... newer and a bit dressier. After dinner all the neighborhood kids came out to play on the sidewalk. Mothers would sit on the front porches for conversation while keeping an eye on the children.

Church has always been a focal point in my family's life. We all attended church every Sunday without fail. Men were leaders in the church. My father's sister's husband was pastor of the church we attended, Fifth Baptist Church. The building was located just a few blocks from where we lived. My father was the Chair of the Trustee Board and my mother's brother was the clerk of the Church. My great-grandparents were founding members and I continue to be a member of Fifth Baptist Church.

Generally speaking, we lived in a separate bubble, as did our white counterparts.

Conflict occurred when these two bubbles intersected, although we rarely encountered whites. A few exceptions:

The white insurance man made his monthly rounds to collect the 25 and 50 cent life insurance premiums. He was brazen, rude and called our parents by their first names, even though they were much older. I hated when he would walk into our home without invitation and would help himself to candy and food without asking.

The Jewish family owned the corner store where we shopped. Often our purchases were placed "on the books" (credit) which never seemed to balance.

Black boys in our neighborhood would take the short cut though Monroe Park on their way home from school. White boys who lived near there always wanted to start a fight. Ironically, unlike today's violent confrontations on the news, in those days no one got seriously hurt and black boys joked, among themselves, about who won or lost.

With those few exceptions, we were isolated from and naive about racism's existence.

The one thing that stood out for me was that men and women and children had clear roles in all families. Children were nurtured in protected environments, and the man's authority as the head of the household was very clear.

My father's voice and discipline was different and dramatic. The authority of his presence was simply commanding and gave us a sense of security. I recall on one occasion while I was in college, I was distraught over what I thought was my boyfriend's cheating on me. I was attending the local historically Black college, Virginia Union University, and was staying off campus, at home. I came home one evening, ran to a room I shared with my sister and threw myself across my twin bed crying profusely. My father heard me through the walls of an attached house he was renovating at the time. I didn't know he could hear me until I heard him coming up the stairs to my room. I thought he was coming to console me. Instead, he asked "what was wrong" in a rather firm voice. I told him I thought my boyfriend was seeing someone else. I thought he was to put his arms around me. Instead he took me by the shoulders and said: "Let me tell you one thing. Don't you ever cry over any man."

The reality lesson my father taught me was worth more than gold. He helped me to see my worth and taught me who I was in relationship to all men. Only a father can teach his daughter such lesson. The same boyfriend has been my husband for more than 52 years.

Without question, my father was the head of our household as were all the husbands in my community. I am a strong, independent Black woman because of my fathers' presence. My husband continues, as my father had, to be the head of the household. He is also a Baptist minister and has been pastor of Third Union Baptist for 45 years.

As I grew older my naivety soon changed. I faced the cold harsh reality of the inequities and cruelties of racism. My eyes were opened to the unjustified separateness where side by side water fountains and public rest rooms were labeled "For Colored Only" and the other labeled "For White Only." Black people were not allowed to try on clothes in Downtown Department stores before purchasing them nor were they allowed to return items for any reason. I came to realize that I lived in an all-Black neighborhood not by choice but by design. I learned about "Redlining" which was the rule of the day where realtors steered black renters and homebuyers to separate neighborhoods declaring that mixing of neighborhoods with Blacks would cause property values to go down.

2

The Betrayal

The situation at Pilanesberg Reserve with the orphaned elephants wasn't over when Tom Thumb was spared. Another teen-aged elephant named Mafuta began causing trouble at a private game reserve near the park. Mafuta turned the reserve's elephant herd, all of whom were orphans relocated without adults, into a street gang. He became the gang leader.

Officials there wanted to provide some discipline to young elephants rather than shoot them and believed separating the young elephants from the adults were a human error. They felt obliged to try to solve the problem before shooting the animals.

At first the scenes seemed funny enough: One day, Mafuta hosed down a rhino with his trunk. But the attacks became more violent. At one point Mafuta spent seven hours stubbornly going after a group of rhinos. When the ranger briefly managed to distract the elephant, the rhinos ran for cover. But when Mafuta saw what had happened, he charged off in a rage. Several weeks later he attacked one of the same rhinos again.

After two more attacks by Mafuta, the gang leader elephant was shot.

"I wasn't happy," the ranger said. "I realized it had to be done, but because I had been working rather closely with the animal, you form emotional attachments."

The people at Pilanesberg also hadn't wanted to kill all the delinquents. After studying the animals, and before they finally decided to euthanize the delinquents, rangers noticed the elephants who were picking on rhinos were suffering from an excess of testosterone. And the youngsters were attempting to mate at an early age because they couldn't handle those raging hormones. They decided to bring in some even larger bull elephants.

Killings at South Africa's Pilanesberg Wildlife Reserve by the orphaned male elephants without male role models began when the pachyderms became teenagers. The elephant kingdom has a complex social system. The female elephants are at the head the pack. This is called a Matriarch system. The female determine where and when the pack will travel, where they will rest or drink water. The young elephants, both male and females stay close in the matriarch pack where they are nurtured and protected by the female head. She will go to extremes to protect her young.

The female elephant stays with the pack for life, but the male elephant gets put out of the pack around the age of puberty. He is then picked up by an older adult bull elephant to mentor (teaching a male elephant how to be a real Bull elephant).

Adult bull elephants cycle in and out of a physical period called *musth*, a time of heighten sexual arousal manifesting increased aggressiveness. The males during this period exhibit liquid drippings and testosterone levels are as much as 60 percent higher than when they are out of *musth*. The young male elephants transported in the reserve without adults, experienced *musth* without the normal intervention of adult Bulls to keep them in line by sparing with them, showing them who's the boss-easing them through *musth*. In the case of the orphan elephants, no big bulls mentored the wild teenagers-during their precocious *musth*. The out-of-control aggression led the young bulls to exhibit deadly force toward the rhinos and other animals in the park. In hindsight, the program, although well intended, created a generation of traumatized male orphans thrown together without adults guidance or behavior training. These orphaned elephants had been betrayed by poor decision making from an administration which did not take into account the complexity of the elephant' species social structure.

Thirty years after the original decision was made to kill the adult and transport the baby orphans, a determination was made to restore the species natural balance. Adult bull elephants were transported to oversee the orphan elephants, a monumental undertaking. Park rangers followed the activity and the interaction of the transplanted adult bulls.

In 1998, rangers from Kruger National Park brought in big elephants in specially designed trucks. No one had ever tried to move elephants that large before.

The bigger, older elephants established a new hierarchy, in part by sparring with the remaining younger elephants to discourage them from being sexually active. That meant less testosterone — good news for the rhinos.

The juveniles seemed to be reading the message loud and clear. Since the big bulls arrived, no rhinos had to been killed. Even Tom Thumb calmed down. He stopped harassing the rhinos, and the rangers hope that when he finally mates, he'll be a new man.

Van Dyk compared it to teenagers acting up who are confronted by their fathers.

"When he gets back to that position, hopefully he's had time to reflect on his misspent youth and think, 'Well I'm big enough to cope with these females, and rhinos are just not an option anymore.'"

The animals' story has an overwhelmingly uncanny similarity with our current issues of violence with the inner city youth.

Just as in the case of the elephants in the jungle, problems in our urban communities have manifested with increased violence. In both the jungle and the urban wilderness, the problems require a remedy. As in the elephant story, the urban problem calls on authority to undo a man-made problem which threatens the well-being of the community.

There Was a Move to Change Old Ways

To understand our current dilemma of uncontrolled violence, we also have to go back in time, as in the elephant story.

The 1960s, more than 50 years ago, our country gave birth to the greatest social and sexual revolution of the century. Break-outs occurred on all fronts, from Women's Liberation to Anti-war Movements and to Civil Rights Protests.

Free Love along with the introduction of birth control pills was the order of the day.

Documented by Stan Busby his book *The Making of a Nation*, the 1960s began with the election of the first president born in the twentieth century — John Kennedy. For many Americans, the young president was the symbol of hope for the nation. When Kennedy was murdered in 1963, many felt their hopes died too-especially young people and of members and supporters of minority groups.

A time of innocence and hope soon began to look like a time of anger and violence. Americans protested to demand an end to the unfair treatment of black citizens. More protested to demand an end to the war in Vietnam; and still more protested to demand full equality for women.

During the '60s the nation went through dramatic upheavals which changed the fabric of the family forever, from the shifting of family roles (the acceptance of men being house-husbands) to a sexual revolution of free love and an "if it feels good do it" philosophy.

In this era, Dr. Martin Luther King led a nation of Blacks into non-violent protests against discrimination, racism and poverty. The period of social unrest changed this nation forever.

With the election of John F. Kennedy, as the youngest President in the history of our country, came a man with liberal ideologies. He believed the government's means and resources could be used to cure the social ills of his time. His views disturbed both extreme conservatives in Congress and white Americans around the country. I was in my senior year at Maggie Walker High School, and remember how excited I was to hear President Kennedy's eloquent speeches. They made me feel like we were on the threshold of obtaining real justice for Blacks.

On June 11, 1963, President Kennedy made one of the most ground-breaking speeches of our times. It was on the heels of Alabama's Governor George Wallace's bold protest against two African-American students attending Alabama State University. Wallace stood in front of the university's doorway to block them from entering the school. An angered Kennedy had to send Alabama's National Guard to escort the students into the school.

Although this speech was made more than fifty years ago, its moral position still holds merit today. The context of the speech is so relevant to the issues currently plaguing our country. The words impacted me and should be repeated as a reminder of the truths it holds today.

Here's what Kennedy said:

"This afternoon, following a series of threats and defiant statements, the presence of Alabama National Guardsmen was required on the University of Alabama to carry out the final and unequivocal order of the United States District Court of the Northern District of Alabama. This order called for the admission of two clearly qualified young Alabama residents who happen to have been born Negro. That they were admitted peacefully on the campus is due in good measure to the conduct of the students of the University of Alabama, who met their responsibilities in a constructive way.

I hope that every American, regardless of where he lives, will stop and examine his conscience about this and other related incidents. This nation was founded by men of many nations and backgrounds. It was founded on the principle that all men are created equal, and that the rights of every man are diminished when the rights of one man are threatened. Today we are committed to a worldwide struggle to promote and protect the rights of all who wish to be free. When Americans are sent to Vietnam or West Berlin, we do not ask for whites only. It ought to be possible, therefore, for American students of any color to attend any public institution they select without having to be backed up by troops.

It ought to be possible for American consumers of any color to receive equal service in places of public accommodation, such as hotels and restaurants and theaters and retail stores, without being forced to resort to demonstration in the street. It ought to be possible for American citizens of any color to register and to vote in a free election without interference or fear of reprisal. It ought to be possible, in short, for every American to enjoy the privileges of being American without regard to his race or his color. In short, every American ought to have the right to be treated as he would wish to be treated, as one would wish his children to be treated. But this is not the case today.

The Negro baby born in America today, regardless of the section of the nation in which he is born, has about one half as much chance of completing high school as a white baby born in the same place on the same day, one third as much chance of completing college, one third as much chance of becoming a professional man, twice as much chance of becoming unemployed, about one seventh as much chance of earning $10,000 a year or more, a life expectancy which is seven years shorter, and the prospects of earning only half as much.

This is not a sectional issue. Difficulties over segregation and dis-crimination exist in every city, in every state of the Union, producing in many cities a rising tide of discontent that threatens the public safety. Nor is this a partisan issue. In a time of domestic crisis men of goodwill and generosity should be able to unite regardless of party or politics. This is not even a legal or legislative issue alone. It is better to settle these methods in the courts than on the streets, and new laws are needed at every level, but law alone cannot make men see right. We are confronted primarily with a moral issue. It is as old as the Scriptures and is as clear as the American Constitution.

The heart of the question is whether all Americans are to be afforded equal rights and equal opportunities, whether we are going to treat our fellow Americans as we want to be treated. If an American, because his skin is dark, cannot eat lunch in a restaurant open to the public, if he cannot send his children to the best public school available, if he cannot vote for the public officials who represent him, if, in short, he cannot enjoy the full and free life which all of us want, then who among us would be content to have the color of his skin changed and stand in his place? Who among us would be content with the counsels of patience and delay?

One hundred years have passed since President Lincoln freed the slaves, yet their heirs, their grandsons, are not fully free. They are not yet freed from the bonds of injustice. They are not yet freed from social and economic oppression. And this nation, for all its hopes and all its boasts, will not be fully free until all its citizens are free. We preach freedom around the world, and we mean it, and we cherish our freedom here at home; but are we to say to the world, and, much more importantly, for each other, that this is a land of the free except for the Negroes; that we have no second-class citizens except Negroes; that we have no class or caste system, no ghettos, no master race, except with respect to Negroes?

Now the time has come for this nation to fulfill its promise. The events in Birmingham and elsewhere have so increased the cries for equality that no city or state or legislative body can prudently choose to ignore them. The fires of frustration and discord are burning in every city, North and South, where legal remedies are not at hand. Redress is sought in the streets, in demonstrations, parades, and protests which create tensions and threaten violence and threaten lives.

We face, therefore, a moral crisis as a country and as a people. It cannot be met by repressive police action. It cannot be left to increased demonstrations in the streets. It cannot be quieted by token moves or talk. It is a time to act in the Congress, in your state and local legislative bodies and, above all, in all of our daily lives. It is not enough to pin the blame on others, to say this is a problem of one section of the country or another, or deplore the facts that we face. A great change is at hand, and our task, our obligation, is to make that revolution, that change, peaceful and constructive for all. Those who do nothing are inviting shame as well as violence. Those who act boldly are recognizing right as well as reality.

Next week I shall ask the Congress of the United States to act, to make a commitment it has not fully made in this century to the proposition that race has no place in American life or law. The federal judiciary has upheld that proposition in the conduct of its affairs, including the employment of federal personnel, the use of federal facilities, and the sale of federally financed housing. But there are other necessary measures which only the Congress can provide, and they must be provided at this session. The old code of equity law under which we live commands for every wrong a remedy, but in too many communities, in too many parts of the country, wrongs are inflicted on Negro citizens and there are no remedies at law. Unless the Congress acts, their only remedy is in the streets.

I am, therefore, asking the Congress to enact legislation giving all Americans the right to be served in facilities which are open to the public -- hotels, restaurants, theaters, retail stores, and similar establishments. This seems to me to be an elementary right. Its denial is an arbitrary indignity that no American in 1963 should have to endure. But many do. I have recently met with scores of business leaders urging them to take voluntary action to end this discrimination, and I have been encouraged by their response. In the last two weeks over seventy-five cities have seen progress made in desegregating these kinds of facilities. But many are unwilling to act alone, and for this reason, nationwide legislation is needed if we are to move this problem from the streets to the courts.

I am also asking Congress to authorize the federal government to participate more fully in lawsuits designed to end segregation in public education. We have succeeded in persuading many districts to desegregate voluntarily. Dozens have admitted Negroes without violence. Today, a negro is attending a state-supported institution in every one of our fifty states. But the pace is very slow. Too many Negro children entering seg-regated grade schools at the time of the Supreme Court's decision nine years ago will enter segregated high schools this fall, having suffered a loss which can never be restored. The lack of an adequate education denied the Negro a chance to get a decent job. The orderly implementa-tion of the Supreme Court decision, therefore, cannot be left solely to those who may not have the economic resources to carry the legal action or who may be subject to harassment.

Other features will also be requested, including greater protection for the right to vote. But legislation, I repeat, cannot solve this problem alone. It must be solved in the homes of every American in every com-munity across our country. In this respect, I want to pay tribute to those citizens, North and South, who have been working in their communities to make life better for all. They are acting not out of a sense of legal duty but out of a sense of human decency. Like our soldiers and sailors in all parts of the world, they are meeting freedom's challenge on the firing line, and I salute them for their honor and courage.

My fellow Americans, this is a problem which faces us all — in every

city of the North as well as the South. Today there are Negroes, unem-
ployed — two or three times as many compared to whites — with inad-
equate education, moving into the large cities, unable to find work, young
people particularly out of work and without hope, denied equal rights,
denied the opportunity to eat at a restaurant or lunch counter or go to a
movie theater, denied the right to a decent education ... It seems to me
that these are matters which concern us all, not merely Presidents or
congressmen or governors, but every citizen of the United States.

This is one country. It has become one country because all the people
who came here had an equal chance to develop their talents. We have a
right to expect that the Negro community will be responsible and will
uphold the law; but they have a right to expect that the law will be fair,
that the constitution will be color blind, as Justice Harlan said at the
turn of the century. This is what we are talking about. This is a matter
which concerns this country and what it stands for, and in meeting it I
ask the support of all our citizens."

President Lyndon B. Johnson ushered in new emphasis on poverty

Five months and 11 days later, on November 22, 1963, at 12:40 p.m.,
President J. F. Kennedy (JFK) was assassinated. Like most people, I
remember exactly where I was when the news broke.

I was in the student grill at Virginia Union University where elevator
music would typically be playing. This day music was interrupted with
a news bulletin announcing the horrible news that President Kennedy
had been shot. Shortly a final announcement declared President Kennedy
was dead.

My first reaction was-disbelief; then came a sense of horror, followed
by a feeling of dashed dreams. My hopes for a more just nation had been
killed along with JFK. Needless to say President Kennedy's promises
would initially go unaddressed but they would be soon taken on by the
newly appointed President. Immediately, Vice-President Lyndon Baines
Johnson was sworn in on Air Force One as President. From all accounts,
the new president was a shrewd politician who had his way of getting
what he wanted though congress. Once sworn in, Johnson rolled up his

sleeves and set out to pass legislation promised by Kennedy. Johnson was a complicated man, though he lacked the polished demure of Kennedy. However, he saw the opportunity to-complete Kennedy's promised civil rights legislation as his claim to fame. Johnson at a press conference said his "objective was to create a sense of continuity and unity for the country." *Flawed Giant, Lyndon Johnson and his times 1961 - 1973.*

LBJ set out to finish the job that John F. Kennedy started. Two notable accomplishments which earmarked his Administration were *The War On Poverty* and *The Great Society*. In his first address to the Joint Session of Congress on November 27 1963, just three days after JFK's assassination, President Johnson made the following statements:

"First, no memorial oration or eulogy could more eloquently honor President Kennedy's memory than the earliest possible passage of the civil rights bill for which he fought so long. We have talked long enough in this country about equal rights. We have talked for one hundred years or more. It is time now to write the next chapter, and to write it in the books of law. I urge you again, as I did in 1957 and again in 1960, to enact a civil rights law so that we can move forward to eliminate from this Nation every trace of discrimination and oppression that is based upon race or color. There could be no greater source of strength to this Nation both at home and abroad.

Johnson would go on to obtain the passage of the Civil Rights and the Voting Rights Acts through Congress. He later initiated sweeping legislation for a national social program aimed at curing the social ills caused by racism. This was his Great Society Program. One of Johnson's greatest speeches to Congress was made following the gruesome March on Selma Alabama on March 7, 1965. That day is referred to as "Bloody Sunday."

In the speech Johnson said *"What happened in Selma is part of a far larger movement which reaches into every section and State of America. It is the effort of the American Negro to secure for themselves the full blessings of American life. Their cause must be our cause too. Because it is not just Negroes but really it is all of us, who must overcome the crippling legacy of bigotry and injustice."*

Johnson then raised his arm, emphatically stating *"We must over-come."* Robert Dallek writes in his book *Flawed Giant: Lyndon Johnson and his times, 1961 - 1973:*

"After that pronouncement a moment of stunned silence followed as the audience absorbed the fact that the President had embraced the anthem of the black protest. (We Shall Overcome) The entire Chamber rose in unison applauding, shouting, some stamping their feet, tears rolling down the cheeks of Senators, Congressmen and observers in the gallery moved by joy, elation, a sense that the victor for a change was human decency, the highest standard by which the nation was supposed to live."

Dallek went on to tell now Johnson continued to espouse the plight of Blacks in America in both rhetoric and action. In his Commencement Address at Howard University in 1965, President Johnson referenced material from a report called "The Negro Family: A Case for National Action." The report was written and sent to him by Assistant Secretary of Labor Daniel Patrick Moynihan. Moynihan identified the widening economic gaps between blacks and whites, and identified the need for a stable family as essential to social and economic advancement.

Johnson pointed out Moynihan's assertion that the core of the problem was the "systematic weakening of the Negro males' (as Blacks were called at the time) positions as husbands and fathers.

At one point, Johnson went on to quote Moynihan, "perhaps most important — its influence radiating to every part of life — is the break-down of the Negro family structure. For this, most of all, white America must accept responsibility. It flows from centuries of oppression and persecution of the Negro man. It flows from the long years of degradation and discrimination, which have attacked his dignity and assaulted his ability to produce for his family."

Moynihan further emphasized: "Unless we work to strengthen the family — to create conditions under which most parents will stay together — all the rest: schools and playgrounds, public assistance and private concern — will not be enough to cut completely the circle of despair and deprivation."

This speech could be given at any commencement today and still be relevant. While the conditions are the same since the delivery of that speech there has been a demise of Black men's role in their families. Clearly the tragic truth is, at all economic levels Black men are still the major target of glaring racial discrimination.

Johnson hoped to remedy these conditions with his development of social programs to build up black families. Ironically, the public assistance program under President Johnson's War on Poverty has been the greatest contributor to the dismantling of black families. Aid to Dependent Children (ADC later called AFDC-Aid to Dependent Families)) was created under the 1935 Social Security Act as a part of Roosevelt's New Deal following the Great Depression. This AFDC-Aid program was created and designed to give relief to single poor white women who were expected not to work but stay at home to raise their children. This was the typical model of family life for whites at the time. Because Black mothers were always in the labor force, they were not viewed as eligible for ADC. (Source - Wikipedia) Eligibility for Black women and children came with the Civil Rights Movement and the push from The National Welfare Rights Organization (NWRO). It appeared initially equal access had finally arrived. However, buried in plain sight was an eligibility factor that would destroy Black families for the next five decades — called "The Man in the House Rule." There was The Betrayal.

3

There is No Man is in the House

Under the government welfare program's man-in-the-house rule, a child who otherwise qualified for welfare benefits was denied those benefits if the child's mother was living with, or having relations with, any single or married able-bodied male. The man was considered a substitute father, even if the man was not supporting the child.

The tone and practice of welfare assistance programs shifted to a punitive approach once Blacks became eligible, implying assistance for black children was undeserved. Social workers would spend more time checking the home for signs of a man than they would provide services to the family. Workers checked under beds, in closets, and searched through drawers for signs of males living in the house. One Housing Development Program Administrator told me they even looked for men's footprints in the snow.

Men were forced to make a choice between staying with their family and not getting assistance or leaving to allow the family to receive public assistance. At first, men would hide from social workers, but eventually they moved away from home altogether. Eventually, the men fell for the rope-a-dope. They gave up their manhood in exchange for pennies for their families from the government. Welfare Departments across this nation were by their actions making "family breakups" a condition of receiving public assistance. This rule was ultimately struck down in 1968 by the United States Supreme Court. The Court found the rule contrary to the legislative goals of the Aid to Families of Dependent Children

(AFDC). Although technically, the rule was gone, the punitive spirit of the rule continued to be practiced for generations. The rule's negative effects on Blacks in America have been far reaching.

The course for Black families has to be changed. The direction is for Blacks to take charge of their own destiny. There must be a national movement for Black Americans by Black Americans. Deep within the Black heritage there is wealth. There is gold.

So much of the American culture was built on the backs of African slaves. African Americans literally helped build the White House and at last a Black American has resided in the White House as President of these United States.

American Garrett Augustus Morgan invented the traffic light; African-American George Franklin Grant created the golf tee.

Black Americans have contributed to everything from the immersion into hip-hop by creator Dr. Kool to today's most relied on cellular technology contributed to by Henry Sampson, the man who is credited with creating the cell phone. The list is endless. Come on folks — "Der is gold in dem dere hills."

During the late 50s thru the 60s Martin Luther King and other brave activist worked hard to change the Civil and Constitutional laws which were discriminatory in nature. This was a critical turning point, making it possible for today's generation to take up the mantle and move from a reactive position to a proactive one.

Blacks must move away from the reactive demonstrations where there is the locking of arms together singing "Somebody's Done Us Wrong Song" or responding with violence, killings, burnings and looting.

Wasted energy must be redirected to action, to re-invention of strong leaders. Black males, *especially*, must set a course to plot their own destiny with positive action and leadership, not destruction and revolt.

Black men must take this responsibility, to rise-up and take their rightful places in productive lives, not by taking out their frustration in violent revolt but by intentional preparation through education, training, and determination.

Black folks are beautiful people, but too many are hidden behind pain.

Their unique hair can be worn in endless styles; the rhythm of their moves and dances are so often imitated; the creativity of their unique attire, and the swagger and the cool male walk.

Yet Black males are far more likely to drop out of school by the eleventh grade and be incarcerated at higher rates.

Unlimited factors contribute to these outcomes including but not limited to: poor educational systems, unprepared for the cultural nuances of economically deprived black males; teachers who fear rather encourage black boys; low educational expectation of black males; lack of black male teachers; high expulsion rates; cultural biases on standardized tests; and general lack of support.

Nevertheless, males are expected to be the leaders.

What is the solution?

Blacks must create their own educational resources, unique to culture and strengths. Churches are the perfect place, with classroom spaces, and retired teachers in the congregation, volunteer tutors, spiritual guidance, and not-too-high overhead-expenses.

Black men and Black women must gain a renewed sense of purpose and independence.

Learning from the orphaned elephants

Similarities between the elephant story and the "War On Poverty" Public Assistance story are astounding.

In both instances authorities made decisions which separated adult males from their off-springs. The actions disrupted a natural socialization process of each species. Both sets of youths acted uncharacteristically violent with tendencies to form gangs. In each instance, the authorities' decisions proved to have devastating results.

To continue the comparison: in both instances, the absence of the adult males who would have tamed the youths proved to have significant and impactful consequences. In the case of the elephants, lack of male role models created out-of- control male adolescents with inappropriate behaviors: premature sexualization and inappropriate killings. In the instance of social-welfare-recipients, the lack of male role models as fathers and husbands left male children in particular prematurely sexualized. The children were also left to make up their own mores and experienced out-of-control violence with high rates of homicides and gang activity.

Some argue "The Man in The House Rule" had unintentional consequences, resulting in an alarming increase in the number of female-headed households.

My belief is the results of the War-on-Poverty arrangement of the mid-1960s were very intentional, and the rule to remove males from the home was a continuation of focused and targeted racial discrimination against black males.

The solution to today's violence is not as simplistic as the animal story. However, restoring the traditional social order of male leadership within families offers a serious beginning.

In 1965, American diplomat, sociologist and politician Daniel Patrick Moynihan predicted the fate of the Black Family in a report called, *The Negro Family: The Case for National Action*. The report focused on the deep roots of black poverty in America. He concluded the relative absence of nuclear families (those having both a father and mother present) would greatly hinder further progress toward economic and political equality. Further, Moynihan's report argued the *matriarchal* structure of black culture weakened the ability of black men to function as authority figures. Moynihan's conclusions met with controversy then, but now this particular notion of black familial life has become widely recognized-as the dominant paradigm when trying to comprehend the social and economic disintegration of late twentieth-century black urban life. (Moynihan, pp. 218–219)

Removing the male head of the household in poor communities was like putting together a football team without a quarterback.

Without leadership, individuals sought self-serving goals, without direction. Households lack order, leaving families scattered and fragmented. With a quarterback, each part of the family would have understood the plays being called and therefore would have known what to do and in which direction to run the ball with combined efforts to achieve a common goal — a touchdown. But instead, with the absence of fathers, Black families have been robbed of common goals and plays to move them to a touchdown. This has led to a moral tragedy.

Shame on you Uncle Sam.

So, let's fix this!

The Human race has been endowed by our Creator with the perfect model of family (mother, father and children) for the purpose of procreation and socialization of off-springs to populate the earth with civil and productive human beings for His Glory. This model cannot be improved upon nor modified to produce the ordained outcomes as planned by the Creator. Our country was founded on spiritual principles from which we have drifted.

In an Article on *Family Values, Race, Feminism and Public Policy,* former assistant U.S. Attorney for the Southern District of New York Twila L. Perry writes:

"In the history of this country, formal public policies and institutionalized racism have acted in tandem to force many black families to develop alternatives to the traditional nuclear family structure."

Cultural Substitutes

Roles such as protector, provider, authority figure, role model, lover, procreator companionship and stabilizer, can be expected where there are male heads of households.

In the poorest communities where public assistance is now a life style because of the welfare system, Uncle Sam assumed the role for most of those concrete or physical sustenance functions as described above with the exception of sex and procreation.

As provider, Uncle Sam supplies monthly income, housing and food stamps. As the protector Uncle Sam provides police to handle domestic disputes and violence. Family court determines paternity and custody, and levies protective orders. Uncle Sam uses Child Protective Services

(CPS) to do its best to insure children remain physically and emotionally unharmed.

For those external laws which substitute for household rules and family discipline, Uncle Sam uses curfews, school suspensions and juvenile detention. Uncle Sam cannot adequately substitutes for parents for any of these family roles. And Uncle Sam should not ever even have attempted to do so. House and family rules and regulations are roles for parents.

I can recall in my household when I was a child, misbehavior at school resulted in consequences at home as well, for poorly representing the family. The same was true in the homes of my friends. Reference was often made to misbehaving children, as acting as if they had "no home training."

The structure of the family is not defined by racial or cultural designation. Roles are deeply rooted and defined by the scripture beginning with Adam and Eve.

Uncle Sam makes a poor "Baby Daddy" when it comes to substituting for a husband and father's role in the family. The term "Baby Daddy" originated with the onset of socially acceptable out-of-wedlock births.

New language cropped up to describe the relationships of out-of-wedlock children and their parents "Baby Daddy" and "Baby Mama," implying these relations were not legitimized by marriage.

Therefore to say Uncle Sam makes a poor "baby daddy" implies the government's illegitimate relationship with women on public assistance has been both irresponsible and life altering.

No welfare plan should oust Black males from the family, leaving the household without a head.

If a man is the leader of his home, he is more likely to take on leadership roles in his neighborhood, his communities, his state, and ultimately his country. The only ones who benefit from the reduction of Black male leadership potential are those who don't want to change the status quo.

When we examine the racial economic hierarchy in the United States of America between blacks and whites, excluding all other racial groups, the white male is at the top of the economic pyramid. The next level is the white female, then the black female and, last, the black male.

As we move further back in American history to the institution of slavery, where blacks were declared property, the idea a black male was equal to a white man was preposterous. Yet, if males in our society are all held to the standard as primary bread winner, why would the black male be at the bottom of the economic pyramid? This is no accident.

The sentiment of white privilege is still alive and well with some in the establishment. And those who hold the sentiment wish to maintain the status quo. They work hard toward eliminating potential competition of any gender or of any other color.

Peggy McIntosh, Associate Director of Wellesley College Center for Research on Women, wrote an essay on white privilege and white male privilege. In her writings, McIntosh acknowledges, as a white person, she was taught about racism as something which puts others at a disadvantage — but not to see white privilege as a consequence of racism. She says she recognizes this would naturally put white folks at a point of advantage.

Further McIntosh says, "I think whites are carefully taught not to recognize white privilege in general, as white males are taught not to recognize male privilege."

One pinnacle point in her article: privilege carries with it an invisible knapsack of unearned assets and power. Expecting white men to share such power and assets, it is my belief, creates a tremendous fear of diminished capacity of power and privilege.

It follows then, white men would not encourage economic and political leadership among black men. This is far from being a new concept. Fear grips top whites with worries about falling off the wall like Humpy Dumpy, never to be put back together again. Fear grips whites at the bottom who would never be able to compete with blacks if the playing field were leveled.

Therefore, the government created a punitive system of public assistance, where the basis of eligibility is absence of a bread winner from the Black family. Absence was ensured by investigations, home searches and midnight raids. Rather than providing support and assistance to impoverished men to enable them to care for their own families, their removal was accomplished.

The thrust of my suggested solution is not to create schism in the body of the Lord's people, but to build up all of His sons and direct them to become the leaders He intended them to be — the Head not the Tail.

Fathers were not seriously sought for child support much of my work era (1970-1996). While laws were in place earlier, the practice of pursuing child support came later.

The worker would ask, "Do you know who the father is? The mother would simply answer, "No." That was the end of the discussion.

Separated from their God given purpose as the head, Black men associated with public assistance cases shifted into a life of aimless living without purpose. The functional needs of caring for family were taken up by the government. Uncle Sam became the provider. While Uncle Sam provided shelter food and clothing, the emotional needs of love, committed companionship and marriage went unmet. Unmarried women were left deprived and emotionally handicapped. Impoverished Black men were intentionally socially and shamefully castrated while white men of privilege were given clear advantages.

Love was replaced with fear. Fear is selfish, violent, defensive and self-serving. Love, therefore is the solution. Love is unselfish, non-violent, supportive and giving. God's plan based on love is perfect for the assigned gender role in the family and not designated for a particular race, creed or religion.

Dr. Wade Horn was President of the National Fatherhood initiative in Gaithersburg, Maryland, when I met him during the late 1990s. Horn came at my invitation to him to speak at Mosby Middle School about fatherhood.

Mosby was one of the toughest middle schools in Richmond and was later rebuilt and re-named Martin Luther King Middle School. The School was surrounded by a public housing complex. City Manager Robert Bobb had formed a new Department of Juvenile Justice Services which launched a grant-funded program designed to reduce the criminal behavior of juvenile repeat offenders. My job was to head up this program. Needless, to say, there were no fathers in the home of these delinquents.

By inviting Dr. Horn, I thought, might empower both the fathers and the mothers to maintain control over the behavior of their own children. The typical approach for Social Service Agencies was to attempt to fix the child through programming and then send the child back to the same home environment.

Still no father! Without exception there were no fathers. Boys could not be retrained to grow into manhood without a man to teach him to respect authority. The Department of Social Services did not serve men.

So, with welfare reform, the government was beginning to encourage fatherhood involvement.

Dr. Horn had moved from the National Fatherhood Initiative to serve from 2001 to 2007 as the Assistant Secretary of the Department of Health and Human Services. Horn ran the Administration for Children and Families (ACF), which administered the Temporary Assistance for Needy Families (TANF, or welfare), Head Start, Low- income Home Energy Assistance Program (LIHEAP), and the Social Services Block Grant (SSBG) programs.

While he was in office Dr. Horn brought his perspective for the need for father involvement to the government. He began to promote and budget for fatherhood programs for the sake of children. These were fragmented approaches which missed curing the core of the problem — broken families.

The whole man in all his roles, especially the role of husband as head of the household within the context of his marriage, was never encouraged. Though Dr. Horn came to recognize these factors at the end of his tenure, Uncle Sam never "really" got behind the promotion of marriages.

Seeking solutions!

Strategies to remove the men were, and are still in full play. As long as black men are not in their correct places, they are not a threat to the status quo. They are not in the game. They are not competitors. Uncle Sam said, "Don't worry, I will take care of your women and children. We got this."

Poverty for children cannot be cured by serving the needs of children alone. Permanent solutions to poverty come with a "hands up approach" for parents. Doors must be opened for fathers of children in poverty to be the bread winners for their families, not Uncle Sam. The solution is a family matter. Uncle Sam can't nurture, love, or raise boys to be men. Too often young Black males, like in the young orphaned elephants in the preserve, lack male authority figures in the family. Outside male authority figures, like mom's boyfriend and the police are often resented by black boys without biological fathers.

Folks are motivated to donate funds when shown a "picture" photo of a starving child. The same people are hard-pressed to contribute to permanent solutions to assisting young fathers, especially Black fathers.

The solution to reducing poverty and violence is staring Uncle Sam right in the face — but it's the elephant in the room.

Black men must be restored to their rightful place as heads of households. Uncle Sam removed the black men and now Uncle Sam must take on the obligation to restore them to their homes where the can be the responsible providers and protectors, with a job with decent wages and real opportunities for advancement.

Uncle Sam must find a way to give all men, regardless of the color of their skin, equal and unalienable rights with equal opportunities for earning comparable wages for him to protect and provide for their families. Stem the tide of ever increasing female heads of household.

Men typically define themselves by both their occupation and roles they play within their families and society. Male children brought up without this model, repeat what they live. Mothers no matter how hard they try, cannot teach a boy to be a man. Emotional mothers raise emotional men.

Black women in low-income communities are themselves broken because of the lies, betrayals and abandonment by men. Low-income single women left to care for the children alone tend to be less demonstrative and have less patience with their children. They are frequently over-burdened with meeting their own emotional needs, so their child's emotional needs go unmet. Unchecked young men in an urban jungle are unleashed to impregnate teen girls without social consequences or condemnation. Society must return to the place where it is not acceptable to impregnate women and walk away.

When a mother abandons her baby after birth, it is considered a crime punishable under the law. Yet if a father abandons his baby after birth, he is not punished for a crime. Yet there *is* a moral crime.

"Black lives matter" at conception, long before grown angry blacks are confronted by the police. The value of a life is defined by how high or low something or someone is regarded. Black babies have been abandoned at birth at alarming rates without regard. Nationally, more than 70% of African-American babies are born without a father listed on their birth certificate. While mothers are also contributors to these statistics, low value to the child's well-being at birth in these cases, is a major contributor. Too often, children are viewed as bi-products of broken relationships and therefore the child's well-being takes a back seat to the emotional trauma between the couple.

The satellite Social Service building where I worked was located in the East End of Richmond, where four Housing Developments for indigents were located in one geographical area. Within the building at that time, my administrative office was located just outside its waiting room. I overheard mothers as they cared for their children while waiting to keep appointments with their caseworkers.

If a little girl hurt her knee, the mother picked the little girl up and pampered her as she cried. But if a male child would fall, the mother would typically scold the little boy, not nurture him as she did the female child. The young boy was told to "shut up" and was offered no comfort. Mothers were trying to make their sons tough and not make a "sissy" out of him. Similar scenarios played out every day, over and over again.

This lack of nurturing of male children set them on a collision course of lacking empathy and compassion. I gained insight into the attitudes of these impoverished mothers. They ascribed the adult male role to their sons. Additionally, in the mothers' minds, comforting young males would make the boys soft, and they didn't want their sons to be soft or become gay.

Male infants are dressed as little men, with the latest pairs of tennis shoes, baseball caps and jeans. And young mothers don't allow their infants to be babies very long but quickly ascribe to them adult attributes beyond their chronological years. Male children in the community tend to be prematurely emancipated as little men by the age of 10 or 11. Many male children are allowed to stay out on their own, left to their own decision of when to come home. On the other hand, female children are kept closer to home for fear of early pregnancy. In the same effort to give them early adulthood, girls are given chores, yet boys are free of such work.

Due to the absence of any permanent adult male presence in the home, a woman tends to call her male off-springs "man- of-the-house." And in many cases, the young men have taken on inappropriate authority such as ordering his mother around, using abusive language with her, or even using physical violence. Some mothers are afraid of their sons and surely unable to discipline them. This is why troubled male children don't follow the same rules as females and won't be told what to do.

This is the tragedy. Nobody can tell boys, who think they are men, what to do. The situation leaves boys with no true male authority or role models in their lives.

Another consequence of the situation results in female loneliness, causing a lack of appropriate choices in dating behavior or practices. Typically, no grown males in the community have their own permanent residences. They tend to stay with their latest girlfriends or with their mothers or grandmothers.

The men are not only looking for a place to stay but also are on the prowl for sex. Children are exposed to many men coming and going. Anxious to have a man in the house, females give these visitors privileges in their homes to which they are not entitled. The visitors have no official position in the home yet are allowed to discipline the children, are given food first, are allowed to place demands on the female and have say-so in regards to the running the home. Older male children, in particular, resent the position the female has given to this non-relative male and more anger grows.

The Intact Family is the Cosmos of the Universe

The nuclear family was carefully crafted into a perfect design by the Creator. The family is the single most influential institution in the world. The home of a family is the place in which the human race is born and socialized. Home is the first seat of civilization.

Prior to the 1960s families across the country were very traditional. The mother's role was very clear as the home maker, taking care of the children and the home. Fathers were the bread winners, being the primary income earners for the household. In white families, females often were more often stay-at-home moms, while in black homes more females worked either outside the home or subsidized household incomes by taking in such work as laundry or ironing. The household, as functional families, did what they needed to do to raise their families.

Today as family roles have evolved, ascribed roles are less rigid in their delineation. While in many instances, this flexibility has been positive, and in other instances, it has muddied the waters.

Orlando Patterson of Harvard University writes in his book *Rituals of Blood:* "African-Americans are the most un-partnered racial group in the United States and perhaps the world." Patterson goes on to say "perhaps the most important group specific problem is the fact that the roles of father and husband are very weakly institutionalized, possibly the worst heritage of the slave past. This is not to say that African-Americans don't value or idealize marriage or partnering (However) idealizing does not mean that one has the means or commitment to achieve it. African-

American males had their culture scripts for the roles of fathers and husbands destroyed both during slavery and ill scripted laws that these men were never quite able to overcome."

"In communities where the socialization of males is lost due to the lack of male role models, and where there is a predominance of female heads of households, one will find negative consequences and development of destructive behavior. These conditions are evident in both urban and rural communities throughout the United States."

Our needed response to the condition is to focused training, education and programming on addressing problems caused by the low percentage of married families in the Black community and the high incidence of fatherlessness resulting in overwhelming social ills.

Black males must now be intentionally bought back to their families with assistance from major resources through local and national efforts. Without a male authority figure in the home teaching respect for civil obedience, guiding and enforcing rules and regulation especially for males, we are headed toward a ruthless society, which has already become evident.

While the United States was founded on Judeo-Christian principles and remains home to more Christians than any other country, the country has become less religious. The Pew Research Center reported Americans describing themselves as Christians dropped from 78 percent to 71 percent between 2007 and in 2014, the number of atheists, agnostics, and those of no faith grew from 16 percent to 23 percent.

According to the 2016 U.S. Census, marriage rates among all races have been in steady decline — in particular Black Americans dropped 29 percent from an all-time high of 80 percent in 1890.

Presently in the US, about 72 percent of Black children are born to unmarried mothers.

The share of young black men without jobs in the U.S. has always been at an unacceptable level. However, according to the 2016 Census, the unemployment rate for Blacks was at an all-time low. This appears to be good news.

However, these figures are problematic because there are multiple sources used in calculating the two figures. The U.S. Bureau of Labor Statistics (BLS) collects data from several different sources to determine both the labor market and the number of unemployed. Some comes from the Census and some from the government unemployment offices.

The figures do not tell the whole story because the low-wealth Black male population is least likely to be counted in either one of these sources in particular.

The BLS determines how the unemployment rates are calculated. The formula uses the number of people recorded to be gainfully employed (Labor Force) divided by the number of people defined to be unemployed. This determines the unemployment rate.

At the end of December 2017, the lowest recorded rate of Black unemployment was 6.8 percent, and the number continues to lower. The positive direction for Blacks still positions the black- unemployment rate far above white people at 2.5% in the same year.

A segment of Black men are not accounted for in the government's statistics — a sort of undeclared homeless population. The average man in this situation would be between the ages of 18 and 45 years, still in his prime, mentally and physically fit, baby producing and cohabiting with baby-mamas, potential baby -mamas and their own mamas as well as other relatives on a temporary basis. They have neither a permanent address nor a legitimate long term job. Weary of not being hired in per-manent jobs, many use pick-up day-jobs such as temp construction workers or temp mover. Additional income comes from illegal drug activity.

The unaccounted males do not go to government unemployment offices to collect or seek work due to limited job history, criminal records and lack of skills and education.

Neither do they show up in the information given to Census takers, who record them as visitors and not permanent residents in the home.

The usual methods of tracking the homeless population in the Census data is counting individual in shelters, feeding resources, and other service resources. Such methods would not capture these numbers of black undeclared homeless men who fall between the cracks and are not counted at all. Ignoring these individuals obscures the accuracy of the unemployment rate.

The numbers of missing Black men from the count can only be collected if Census takers acknowledge this population exists and if the Bureau initiates a method to include semi-homeless in the count in as they do the totally homeless population.

Comparatively few resources are dedicated to build family capacity toward the fullest potential. United States Constitution, Article One, requires the total population be counted at least once every ten years. This count is used to set the number of members each state will have in the House of Representatives. Article One also determines how $400 billion of Federal funds is allocated to communities and neighborhoods for such things as education, public health, employment, crime and housing.

More detailed surveys are intermittently completed in between the ten year population count to look closer at such areas as economics, consumers, expenditures, local employment etc.

The method and breakdown for distribution of Federal funds to a community is determined from these statistical analyses. For this reason these statistics must be accurate and counting every person is critical. In this instance, the most-needed data in building family capacity, is the least likely to be counted.

A *2018 Kids Count* data book released by the Casey Foundation predicts the 2020 census could be mired in challenges which might shortchange the official census count by at least one million kids under 5 years old. This would underfund critical federal dollars needed as resources for family stability.

Church and state constantly make reference to the importance of family but only giving lip service to the significance. Churches, agencies and organization do not put money behind solutions to the problem of the semi-homeless males who have gone missing from their families. America has lost all priorities for shaping and educating the minds of young people affected by absent fathers.

Misplaced priorities have led to giving higher value to sports than shaping the minds of young people who will populate the future. Within 40 states, college coaches earn higher salaries than the University Presidents. The University of Louisville paid its men's basketball head coach $6.1 million for the 2010/2011 season. In contrast, the President of the University of Louisville made $456,132 in 2010. More resources are put into the sports we treasure but not into nurturing the minds and character of human capital within the context of intact families and our educational institutions.

America can no longer afford to leave family development to chance. People must intentionally, with all deliberate speed, invest in the entire family as a unit.

In the case of the Black male, absence from the family is quite evident in incident involving police and community destruction. Government programs such as "Maternal and Child Health," Child Welfare Services, Male Health, and Fatherhood Programs concentrated on fragmented pieces of the family puzzle. These splintered programs have failed to serve the entire family. If the father is not present, a system should be established to go get him and then serve the family as a unit to encourage keeping the members together.

In the beginning, the Creator designed family as an intact unit the perfect design which cannot be modified or redesigned to satisfy contemporary definitions. Females alone cannot alone raise a boy to be a well-balanced man without the influences of other men. Males alone cannot raise girls to be balanced women without input from other females. The Creator's design calls for input from both genders in order to produce balanced individuals. This is not an indictment on the millions of women who have been forced to raise their children alone.

Men and women are formed physically to accomplish their prescribed roles. She was designed to have babies, to be the nurturer — the keeper of emotions, the sentimental one, and the glue hold everyone together. She makes the house a home and is the primary caretaker, but she can only accomplish this if the primary roles of her husband are also met. She is a perfect fit with the male both physically and spiritually.

The male is built for physical strength and spiritually crafted to protect and provide for his family. He is driven by his purpose to be the leader of the pack. His position gives him pride, drive and inspires him. The male psyche tends to be goal-driven and functional, not to the exclusion of appropriate emotionalism, while the female is more emotional but not to the exclusion of the ability to be functional. Of course each gender has some of each attribute.

For the purpose of this discussion, these definitions are offered:

Emotional Orientation is defined as self-directed feelings, commonly lacking rational influence. Emotionally oriented people have feelings of urgency with the drive toward action without the consideration of outcomes or the ability to delay gratification. These feelings, such as revenge or pleasure, require immediate satisfaction. Exacerbated by stress, these feelings are self-serving with little consideration of or for others, or for the potential consequences to self or others.

With the current preponderance of female heads of households in low-income communities, children are reared primarily from a female emotional orientation without the balanced contribution of the male's functional influence. While males are also innately aggressive, women are innately emotional. The way she raises her children typically has a heavy emotional orientation. Values and priorities in the household are driven by emotional undertones, exacerbated by stress and over-burdened conditions.

If females are raising all of the males in the community, the entire community takes on emotional responses to stimuli. For example, if a man is offended by another, his first reaction is to seek immediate emotional revenge with a desire for immediate gratification. Added to the natural aggression of males, he is more likely to be violent without consideration for the consequences.

In Black neighborhoods, heavy emphasis is placed on external appearances and self-gratification which might make one feel good ... or bad. Material things-and physical appearance hold high value. The standard for giving a sense of affirmation for attractiveness for women is hair, typically weave and artificial nails. Men or women living in an emotional environment are dependent on short term goals and immediate gratification. But, no matter how tough or beautiful or well-dressed or strong a woman is, emotion over circumstances drive her decision-making process when she is acting alone as head of household.

Functional Orientation is an intentional drive to take action with purpose and goals, with an end in mind whether positive or negative. A person with a functional orientation makes decisions based on long-term sense of gratification which can be delayed for higher achievement. Outcomes are considered before taking action. Males are more prone to be innately functional. Traditional family culture ascribe women to child nurturing, an emotional task, while the role of men is ascribed to providing and protecting, a functional task. These roles are definitely not etched in stone and may be reversed in many families. Males who are raised and socialized by a male are more likely to manifest male functional attributes.

Balanced orientation, whether an individual is raised by a male or female alone, refers to a balanced or unbalanced individual when it comes to emotional/functional responses to stimuli. The desired balanced orientation comes with balanced input from both emotional and functional stimuli. Some individuals manifest extremes in functioning. One with extreme unbalanced functional orientation is without balanced input tends to lack empathy, sympathy and romantic consideration. The unbalanced functional person simply wants to reach goal letting nothing get in the way. Extreme, unbalanced individuals tend to exploit others to reach their goals. The extreme unbalanced individual fails to look at goals, outcomes, or consequences. The person with this orientation focuses only on immediate feelings and self-absorption. Little is accomplished for the good of others by someone with this orientation who produces a self-serving environment. Extremists are unable to make sacrifices for the benefit of the children because their needs come first.

In the Creator's design, the nuclear family offers a perfect balance. The presence of both mothers and fathers offer a balance of both functional and emotional orientations working in tandem, congruently. Even with both mothers and fathers present, poor parenting can still occur. The bare basics of the presence of both parents sets the stage and gives the backdrop for raising healthy children who are primed to reach their fullest potential. Anything less starts the child off with a handicap and makes harder for them to achieve.

The Emotional Community:
We Learn What We Live

For almost seventeen years, I worked in the heart of low-income Black communities. The following chapters are my observations of the ever-evolving sub-culture of those neighborhoods.

The low-income communities were predominately matriarchal. The communities were characteristically emotional and feminine in orientation. Men raised by female heads of household, without the influence of male role models, tended to be more emotional.

With emotional orientation, the residents required immediate gratification with little to no long-term planning in place. They tended to work for short-term gain, typically focused on personal or materialistic gratification such as obtaining expensive car-rims, Jordan shoes and other recognized name-brand tennis shoes, jewelry, or name-brand jeans.

Like most women, males in the communities placed high value on shoes, especially tennis shoes. Not just any tennis shoes but brand name, and the latest on the market. Many of these males owned upwards of 20 or more pairs of tennis shoes. Stepping on another man's tennis shoes could get someone killed. High value also is placed on matching outfits as well as clunky gold jewelry. Matching outfits may involve matching colored tennis shoes, shirt, pants and hat or cap.

Work ethics, particularly among this black male population, have evolved poorly in low wealth communities. Temporary work is seen as a means to an immediate end, to quickly acquire those desired material items. Emotional reasons for quitting a job might include such poor excuses such as, "The boss man does not know how to talk to me," – which means the he believes the manger is speaking to him with disrespect. Or "I can't go to work because my girl-friend went in the emergency last night," or "I ain't washing no toilet." Work has no purpose other than satisfying an immediate personal need, not working to care for a family.

Growing up in poverty means making choices between what makes one feel good in the short term or what has long term lasting value. But the impoverished get such little reward on a daily basis, the short-term reward wins out every time.

Men in the community fail to mature. There appears to be a fear of growing up to adulthood. After all, responsible adults are held to higher standards for which they are not prepared to achieve. Therefore, older men tend to dress in the style of the younger guys. They mimic what they perceive to look young, cool, and prosperous without having responsibility — as if they have money with jewelry and luxury cars.

The need is to overcome poor self- esteem. How can a man stand among other men with no legitimate work identity? The first thing a man ask another man, after being introduced is ... "So what is it that you do?" (Meaning: what kind of work do you do, or what is your occupation.) Often in the larger society, the answer to this question is the basis of one's self esteem or identity. For this discounted population, answering this question would not have a feel-good conclusion. For them, the concept one could legitimately work to earn permanent prosperity, appears to be beyond reach.

Work ethics, particularly among the male population, evolved poorly in low wealth communities. Work is seen as a means to an immediate end, to quickly acquire desired material items. Long-term work or holding on to a job for long term purpose is not highly valued. Emotional reasons for quitting a job might include such poor excuses such as: "The boss man does not know to talk to me," or "I can't go to work because my girl-friend went in the emergency last night," or "that kind of work is beneath me." Because they had no real purpose they only concentrated on satisfying their own personal needs and desires.

Growing up in poverty hurts. No one wants to look poor, so the appearance of prosperity has a high value. The need to overcome poor self- esteem doesn't include the idea one could legitimately work and earn prosperity — this concept is not in the daily pyridine of the discounted black males because of racial discrimination and economic indifference. Fast illegitimate money is spent on feel-good items: drugs, alcohol, women and over-priced clothes and shoes.

Having show-off items takes priority over necessities. A mother may be late paying her electric bill so she can buy her child a name brand jacket to wear to school. Money matters, but the idea of having the appearance and flaunting the trappings of wealth as they see it, is giving such mothers a false sense of value. The false symbols of wealth may be such things as luxury cars, fancy jewelry (even-though it looks cheap to the rest of us), vicious dogs, expensive car rims, guns and expensive casual clothes.

Functional planning for necessities such as housing, groceries and transportation goes unattended for the men folks. Girlfriends, mothers or other relatives are expected to provide these necessities. The emotional man looks to be taken care of rather than he being the provider.

Most black men have a swagger in their walk and a ready line. With his cool lines, he can convince any woman, he's the one to take care of them better than their last man. In reality, his motive is to woo her into sex. His concerns are self-absorbed to meet his own needs, whether they are sexual, material or emotional. Sex and procreation are the two roles Uncle Sam left to males living in poverty once he usurped the headship role as the man of the house. Sex subsequently became a poor substitute for love. How can women tell the difference between sex and love when they have never experienced unconditional love of a father?

Despite economic drawbacks, low-wealth women take great pride in their hair and nails, unlike their low-income male counter-parts. Most all women, regardless to racial or cultural orientation, seek to be attractive. The guys gladly pay for their woman's hair and nails as a way to "get some play" (be with her sexually) and these women keep Oriental Beauty

Supply stores located in their communities in business.

The men of the urban maze, like the orphaned elephants, were never socialized to understand their intended purpose, but their purpose must and can be restored through education, training and spiritual support. Women, left abandoned by the biological fathers of their children, are forced to be the more functional of the two procreators. She must make provisions for herself and her family, although, so often she is not fully engaged in the task and is not ready to sacrifice her emotional needs for her children. Her need for companionship may override her patience and physical affection for her children. Having to carry the full burden alone certainly challenges the joy of parenthood.

The Do-Rag

There is an interesting phenomenon when it comes to the do-rag, a cloth used to cover the top of the head sometimes called a skull-cap or a wave-cap, and according to Meriam-Webster derives from 'do as in hairdo.

A common sight in today's "hood," the do-rag serves a purpose deeper than just wrapping up a hairdo. It connects African-Americans to their history.

During slavery, the women tied their hair up into scarves. Later, from the 1930s to the 1960s, the cloths reappeared for both Black men and women. The men used the cloths to hold chemically processed hair-dos in place while they slept.

Homemade "stocking caps" were actually fore-runners to the current do-rags. Prior to the 1960s — and prior to the manufacture of panty hoses — females wore silk or nylon stockings with garters, garter belts, or hooks attached to girdles to-keep them from sliding down ladies' legs. Since the stockings were thigh high and generally very thin, they would easily put a "run" in them.

Women never felt proper to be caught wearing stockings with runs in them but ladies could always use a run-less stocking from another pair to wear, stretching the usage. Women never felt proper wearing stockings with runs, but black men found them useful, a practice, not confined to any particular economic level. The men would use the discarded stocking in the traditional way women used a do-rag. The men would cut the stocking near the double layered thigh part tie a knot to use as a stocking cap. Kinky hair, with the assistance of hair-dressing products, pressed tightly down under this stocking cap and took on a wavy pattern. Most men wore the stocking cap only at night and took it off to show the final look in public during the day. The wavy style was deemed attractive, "good hair," appearing close to whites' hair.

Guys who wore stocking caps in the public all day were considered thugs.

While the trends of black men's hair styles evolved from processed hair, to permanent waves with *Jheri* curls, to dread-locks and braids, so did the practical usages for do-rags. The do-rag relegated itself primarily to young inner-city black males. The ever-popular new hairdo among inner-city black men continued to require upkeep. Between short money and complacency, do-rags were an easy fix for unkempt hairdos and covered needed hair-cuts, braids needing a redo or hair–needing grooming.

Why Do They Do What They Do?

When the "Man in the House Rule" was enforced, if there were a man living in the home whether he was the father of the children or not, the man was declared to be "able bodied" and thus the family was determined to be "Not in Need of Service."

Those black men themselves were living in poverty. While later the rule was struck down as unconstitutional, the sentiment prevailed in practice, continuing to stripping black families of the opportunities to function as a unified family. No help or assistance came from Uncle Sam in the way of employment assistance to help men contribute to their households with encouragement to restore broken families.

In fact, through the '70s, child support was not sought from absent fathers. No emphasis was placed on men being held responsible as providers. Uncle Sam was the provider and kept the Black male away. Home life for many black males became unstructured, even if they had a consistent place to stay. And male children, unlike the girls, were given few chores.

Under the 1986 Welfare Reform Act the Ronald Reagan Administration complained about welfare dependency. This was the same Uncle Sam who, by removing the bread-winner from the home, created the dependency in the first place. The government declared those on public assistance must now go to work when a child turns three.

With the men gone, those on public assistance were predominately mothers. With the rule change, Uncle Sam, put the women to work, giving them job employment preparation, job training and on-the-site job placement. The government did not consider these welfare-children's fathers needed to be trained and placed on a job to take care of their own. The action of the government amounted to "keep them black men-down where they are. Let's not disturb the status quo."

Uncle Sam was keeping the families broken, apart and poor. Further, Uncle Sam's actions threw the poor together in the same pools of low-income housing; corralled them together in neighborhoods like Concentration Camps. The results have left black families in poverty, depressed and angry, without hope.

Sad is the climate where impoverished parents assume their children are going to jail within their life expectancy, while middle class parents assume their children will go to college.

The routine culture of poor neighborhoods is absorbed with anticipation of future incarceration. Jailhouse-type attire such as slide shoes with socks, baggy pants with no belts, white undershirts and sleeveless tee-shirts (referred to as wife-beaters) are common sights in homes and on the streets. The habit of exposing personal under-garments, and the wearing of pajamas, bedroom shoes, in public has become indistinguishable from personal inappropriateness as a learned behavior in jail.

The hopeless have infected a large portion of the black culture to move about as though they suffer from the lack of privacy as if the individuals are already in a jail-house. The black population has been desensitized to personal discretion, brought in by those released from jail, once they are back home in the streets.

What Motivates Human Behavior?

Studies in social sciences and in human behavior have shown, if human²s are to thrive, they require their needs to be met starting from infancy. When individuals' needs are not met, the level of thriving is lessened. A psychologist named Abraham Harold Maslow created a theory of how humans progress through a hierarchy of needs. He suggest humans will move from meeting the lowest levels of needs, the basic need (for food, shelter and water), to building upon the next levels of need, striving to reach the ultimate level to which Maslow calls self-actualization. Maslow suggests the individual will not seek higher levels if lower level needs are not met.

While Maslow's theories have been challenged over the years, his hierarchy of needs did bring attention to the complex needs of humans as to whether or not they thrive.

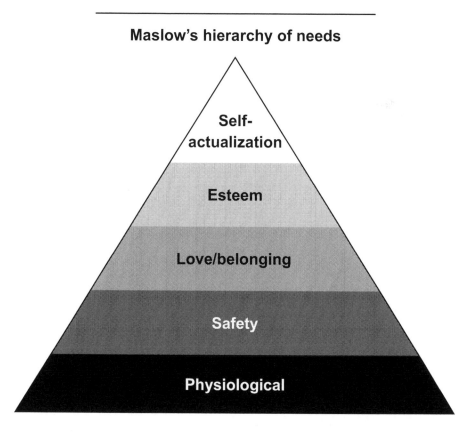

Maslow's hierarchy of needs

Maslow starts with only physical needs at the first level, leaving out social and emotional needs, but this creates some concerns. Studies have shown significant factors affecting the infant's temperament exists as early as in the womb. For example, a study done at the University of Denver by researchers Elsia Poggi Davis and Pilyoung Kim explored how stress affects a baby's brain in the womb. High levels of the stress hormone corisol were found in infants whose mothers had high levels of stress hormones while pregnant. The babies who had high levels of cortisol before birth took longer after birth to comfort when troubled than children who had not been stressed in the womb. The study concluded stress in the womb could have an impact on the child's cognitive ability. Factors affecting children's adjustment to life add challenges for low-income mothers who are at greater risk for high stress levels.

Uncle Sam met the lowest levels of Maslow's defined needs of the Mothers on public assistance: Public housing; food stamps; and a monthly welfare stipend to insure that the basics needs were covered. However, meeting basic needs alone cannot substitute for potential emotional support or distress which could potentially come from a marital partner. Maslow's hierarchy of needs was proposed in 1943. While his work still holds many truths today, psychology has come a long way in understanding human motivation as well as the critical importance of physical touch.

Human touch is as essential as food, water, warmth and rest and should be listed in Maslow's first level of basic needs. The lack of human touch proved to be fatal to many infants during an experiment by Rene Spitz, a psychoanalyst, to lower risk to infants' exposure to hazardous infectious organism.

Spitz studied infants to reduce the incidence of disease he believed to be spread by human contact. This was an unconventional idea in the 1940s, the time of his experiment. To accomplish this experiment, he gathered babies separated from mothers in prison and babies from orphanages to participate in the study.

As a part of the study all of the physical needs of the babies were met. They were fed, clothed, kept clean, warm and dry. However, they were not held or played with, so as not to risk hazardous infectious exposure, Spitz believed. The results were devastating. In spite of meeting the physical needs of the infants, the babies became sick, lost weight and many died.

What was so tragic, the babies were subjected to more infections than the average rate. In one of the institution used in the study, the mortality rate to measles was 40 percent compared to 0.5 percent, the national average rate. Further irony showed a death rate of 75 percent in the cleanest and most sterile institution. Spitz in his investigation showed the lack of the human touch and interaction was life altering. Human touch turned out to be as critical as the air itself.

A baby born outside of wedlock is a tremendous source of stress for any mother, not only to those in poverty. Negative effects from abandonment, non-commitment, and lack of support from fathers cannot be minimized. Expecting babies should be a source of joy and pride for a married couple, binding them together as a family.

Girls wanting a baby to love or a baby to love them — or for a paycheck — are prevailing myths. Babies born to single women in poverty actually result from the female wanting a male's touch, perhaps the touch of love she did not receive from her father — simple temporary physical affection. Babies are the bi-product of an illusion of love.

An old saying: "Men give affection to get sex, and women give sex to get affection." This saying is close to the truth. Lack of touch and affection in one's early development is a formula for life-long disaster.

Wellspring Workbook by Dr. John W. Travis and Regina Sara Ryan contains an article about how the lack of sufficient touch has far-reaching effects on-development and shows itself in problematic ways at maturity. The article suggests some destructive means of compensating for unmet needs of touch:

Overeating — trying to fill an inner void left by unmet oral needs, and deadening the pain of emotional isolation, often through eating fatty foods to envelop empty emotions. In some instances, eating out of bowls like infants are fed instead of eating out of plates like adults.

Self-destructive habits such as smoking, nail-biting, pulling out hair, rubbing the skin excessively, and even self-mutilation.

Compulsive sex, physical violence and aggressiveness, rape, and other forms of sexual abuse.

The article further explains the biggest problems touch deprivation creates are alienation from self and isolation from others manifested in these behaviors:

Boredom with, and lack of energy for, life in general; the experience of being out of touch with or disconnected from the world.

Sexual dysfunction — an unresponsiveness to the special electricity of the touch of another human body; over-anxiousness, which can encourage both premature ejaculation and overall bodily tension; and fear of one's own body.

Unsatisfying relationships, unwillingness to attend to the needs of the other, self-preoccupation, excessive shyness, the fear of reaching out, and the fear of sustained intimacy.

The destructive and negative behaviors , often exhibited by low-income women, gained from the lack of satisfaction in life, leaves them unprepared as single parents to meet…their own emotional needs. The emotional deficit in the women causes them to rush to reduce the child's dependence and to grow them up prematurely. For example, emotionally empty moms will impose adult attributes on the child very early. The mom believes an infant is deliberately crying to make them angry or soiling their diaper on purpose. Mom dresses her babies as miniature adults, forces the little ones to hold their own bottles by propping the bottle up. These detached women seldom hold, or rock, or cuddle their babies, and instead of milk-feeding babies, they give them soft drinks in baby bottles. Toddlers are neglected in harmful ways: little ones' hands are not held by an adult when crossing the street; tots are talked "at" in adult language, including profanity; tots are expected to comply with unreasonable demands for their age. The high intolerance and impatience with childhood by stressed adults, especially with young boys, brings on premature emancipation, with delayed maturity in accepting adult responsibility.

Babies born in poverty today are worse off than others in the past 50 years. The current generation of impoverished babies is not only financially poor but, because of the early welfare "no man in the house" rule, the children are also orphaned. Welfare babies are more likely than their middle-class counterparts to be emotionally abandoned by their mothers and physically abandoned by their fathers; therefore rendering them virtual orphans. These children will more than likely grow up raised on the streets, without male role models to guide and socialize them into responsible adulthood, in the way our orphaned elephants suffered.

Uncle Sam can generally meet Maslow's concrete primary needs, but Uncle Sam makes a poor substitute when it comes to providing touch — the hugs, love and kisses basic to human survival.

In the 21st Century, building sky scrapers is easy. Man went to the moon and space crafts are probing the universe. Endlessly evolving technology has offered man the ability to create a baby in a Petri dish. Understanding of all of human development is studied in America, the most advanced nation on earth, yet ... the American poor people, casted in a schism between the haves and the have-nots put this nation to shame.

6

The Functional Community

Maslow's Second Level of Needs

Maslow's Second Level in his hierarchy is the need for Safety and Security. At the Second Level Maslow contends a responsible adult takes into consideration safety and security for himself and others. This includes personal physical safety, resources, employment, morality, health, family and property.

If persons have not had all of their first level basic needs met, as in the case of virtual urban orphans, second level movement is obscured. Lack of fulfillment takes a toll on the person's ability to recognize the functional needs such as securing a home, income/employment, health, safety and protection in the environment.

When one's emotional needs are unmet a person's ability to look out for the needs of others is severely hampered and compromised forcing a continuous search to fulfill those initial first level needs in Maslow's hierarchy.

For example, instead of the men taking on the role to be the provider of those security factors for his family, because he is shut out of his family by the welfare system rule, he tends to become self-absorbed and narcissistic in meeting his own needs, whether that be for sex, a place to stay, money or other factors.

Why? Not because some genetic abnormality, but because Uncle Sam deprived these men for generations of the natural order of socialization.

Men are naturally aggressive and must be socialized into civil behavior.

Who is Protecting Whom?

For more than 50 years, policies and practices of the government created circumstances which discouraged men in poverty from reaching levels of responsible adulthood. Boys and girls have been robbed of feeling safe and protected by a male head of household. Just the sheer physical presence of a strong man, ready to act in the face of threats, was absent from the family. Instead, their replacements are out-of-control young males who lack moral guidance from responsible adult role models, creating chaos and violence, and turning communities into urban jungles. The similarities easily compare with the orphaned elephants on the preserves.

The adult males, having been shut out of their traditional community role by the welfare rules, dress like teenagers in an effort to extend their youth rather than taking on responsible attributes of adulthood. Women are left to fend for themselves against men who have learned to exploit them rather than protect them.

Women lose their focus as mothers by putting her desire to please the current boyfriend before meeting needs of her own children. For example, boyfriends get fed first and are given the best of the food while the children must fend for themselves of make their own food. Who is making their children feel safe? Who will protect the girls from inappropriate behaviors of the neighborhood thugs? Children learn to resent mama's boyfriends and see these men as takers rather than providers and protectors. This is their model of life.

The truth of the matter is, no one feels safe. The same guys who are perpetuating violent acts are also afraid. They are afraid of being bullied, afraid of retaliation, and afraid of being gotten first. They are always looking over their shoulders. Kids sit in classrooms buried in their coats all day as a way of shielding or protecting themselves from the outside world. The hoodie is another piece of apparel that is used as a hiding device to cover-up or disguise oneself from others in the hood, the police or just to be anonymous.

The leader or family head should set the tone for the family and make the members feel safe and protected. Parents should be good leaders, always ready to sacrifice for the sake of their children regardless to personal cost and delaying personal gratification. When children see the head of the household places child safety and care first, the children feel secure and protected. The problem is, there are few strong family heads who themselves feel safe or fulfilled. Fathers and father accountability are absent by the initial design of the welfare program. Women, often too busy seeking self-gratification, are just trying to make it from day to day with little joy, living through the lives of daytime soap operas and seeking the company of unreliable and sometimes abusive male partners.

Drugs and alcohol are often used to dull the pain for both the women and men of a joyless and lusterless life. Grandmothers often fill in the gap. The likely problem is, she did not raise her own children while she chased an empty dream of a joyless life. Now that she has come in off the street, she is a first-time parenting grandmother with little parent skills of her own.

The ability of a person to become a good family head and leader comes from having felt protected themselves as they grew up. After generations of shaping families under the welfare rules children have grown up to feel less-than protected and more like second-class residents in their own homes, to live-in boyfriends. A nation of American Black men have grown up treated as second-class citizens in their own country, left feeling unsafe and unprotected. The Black male today, after years of the second-class treatment, feel those who are paid to protect the public are more inclined to protect the public from them.

Not to minimize the trauma of abuse imposed upon black males, in particular by police, there is much more to recognizing how "black lives matter." The value of Black lives is extensive, far reaching, and limitless. The value of Black lives is not one dimensional. Black lives, like all lives, matter in totality. High value of life at all levels must be sought and demanded. Value of "life" must be recognized at all levels, from conception, to birth, to the grave. *All life matters.*

The lives of fathers and husbands, as protectors and providers, *matter*.

Yet, there are no Black protesters demanding Black fathers meet critical needs and protection of their own flesh and blood.

No Black protestors are railing with indignation about what *matters* when other Black men are allowed to dishonor their daughters, sisters, mothers and aunties, by impregnating them, abandoning them and their unborn children.

No demonstrators protest when incarceration becomes an expectation in life instead of high school graduation. All purposeful dimensions of black lives should *matter* and be equally valued, guaranteed and protected.

Who Is Creating Leaders As Providers And Protectors?

As early as elementary school, boys raised in poor neighborhood, holding the potential to be the head of their own households and leaders in their communities, tend not to be pushed toward a good education. The youths are mentally dropping out of school by the fifth grade and physically dropping out before graduation. Mothers who share similar poor experiences in school are not generally encouraging.

In the neighborhood culture, parents see their roles as defenders of their children from the teachers, as opposed to partnering with teachers for their children's success.

In my earlier generation parents were great supporters of the teachers. Parents respected and valued the impact teachers would have on their children's development. The combative attitudes of today's parents, coupled with teachers' fears of young black males — especially the fears by young white female teachers — increase odds against black boys reaching their full potential. Normal boy-antics too often draw overreaction, with exacerbated punishment, ending in high suspension, expulsion and drop-out rates.

Black youths struggle along all points of the academic continuum according to a report from *Yes We Can, the Schott Foundation's 50-State*

Report on Public Education and Black Males; A Call for Change, by the Council of the Great City Schools; and *We Dream a World,* by the 2025 Campaign for Black Men and Boys.

Statistics in the February 2011 edition of *Focus on Blacks: Race Against Time: Educating Black Boys* show, with different tools, it is possible to reverse the trajectory of success for economically poor Black boys.

Using a suite of student-centered strategies, a Newark New Jersey principal, named Baruti Kafele of Newark Tech High School transformed his school climate and culture into a productive academic achieving Institution. The student- centered system recognized the individual student from an emotional orientation which had to first be addressed. The impoverished community in its entirety functioned from an emotional orientation. Author Daniel Goleman's book Emotional Intelligence suggests emotional intellect (EQ)is a greater predictor of success than Intellectual Quotient (IQ). Until the community is restored to a balance between functional and emotional orientations, individual safety, advancement, and self-sufficiency will not thrive.

Black and Hispanic students in Newark, New Jersey, called Newark Tech High School, more than 85 percent of the students are poor enough to qualify for free or reduced lunch. Yet, this high school was recognized by *US News & World Report* magazine as the best High School in the Nation. In 2010, 88 percent of the student body tested proficient in math, 100 percent tested proficient in reading, and 100 percent graduated.

Black male students in poverty are more likely to hit the streets than the books. Not because they are intellectually inferior nor because they are poor, but are emotionally bankrupt. Further, black and Hispanic boys are-more likely than white counterparts to be placed in special education, to be suspended from school or to drop out completely.

Newark Tech High, Principal Baruti Kafele recognized academic performance of his students was not in crisis. The students did not have an academic problem, but they were each in self-crisis. Principle Kafele puts it this way:

"Most school systems are addressing this crisis as an academic problem, but these kids are in self-crisis, we can't address a crisis of self-image, self-esteem, self-discipline, and self-respect as an academic problem, and if we keep trying to solve it in terms of math and reading models, ... we'll be reading the same reports (poor statistics) 25 years from now."

Schools have to address the "affective" before they address the academic. "The generic approach isn't working."

The majority of the poor black boys attending school, came from an environment which did not feel it was cool to be academically smart. Kafele transformed the school environment making it cool to soar, applying the following tools:

1. School Leadership: Kafele suggest staff, no matter how well trained, needs the full support of a leader committed to the work of giving special attention to educating these impoverished male youth. Kafele. whose first name is African, meaning, teacher, greets each student at the door as they arrive to school. Each day he gives a positive message over the public address system to counter act negative messages the kids get outside of the school.

2. Male empowerment sessions: Manhood discussions are held, with individuals, in small and in large groups. Men from the community are invited to have frank discussions. Seniors volunteer at elementary schools, demonstrating positive modeling of manhood for young black boys.

3. Culturally responsive schools: First educators must get to know and understand the culture of the students. It must be the responsibility of Universities preparing teachers to include cultural diversity training. Then the teachers must employ this knowledge in culturally responsive curriculum and instructions, acknowledging the students' background, home environment and the impact on student's learning processing. Kafele explains educators focus on wrong measures. Rather than achievement gaps, he suggest educator focus on learning gaps (the reason students are not learning), the attitude gap (the difference between students who believe in themselves and those who don't), the relationship gap(those who have stable relationships with educators and those who don't), the opportunity gap (those who have access to excellent public schools and

those who don't), and the relevance gap (concrete learning materials and lessons students can apply to their daily lives in comparison to lessons which are abstract and intangible.

The principal believed the school had to work on things that "affected" the students to work on their broken spirits.

Educators might say they are not social workers nor were they trained to do that kind of work. But Uncle Sam broke up the students' families, cracking the families into emotional pieces. Water cannot be poured into a broken glass, and expect the vessel would hold it. Educators might say, "That's a home problem and not a school's problem." Teachers may feel their job is to teach students who are ready and willing to learn, but therein lies the problem. Students live in different houses and must be taught according to their life experiences and living conditions. The educators' job is to teach whoever comes to them, wherever they come from just as a doctor would treat patients according to their individual needs.

Generic approaches will not work with students coming from emotionally bankrupt homes.

The approach taken by the Newark Tech High is an excellent example of how school systems can change in their approach to student-centered strategies.

As long as school systems continue their current practices using generic Standards of Learning (SOL) type indicators, and as long as educators refuse to change their teaching styles, results will be the same: high drop-out rates and low graduation rates. Institutions educating teachers must prepare the educators to teach keeping the uniqueness of the children in mind. Teachers unwilling to make the effort should not be hired. Only fully dedicated teachers can help each child reach their fullest potential. Throw away the "idea" schools cannot perform the job without the support of the parents. Students who have no home support system must be approached as orphans. Students who do not have parents' support cannot fit into middle-class school model but focus on the individual student.

The nation must make educating *all* of its future leaders its highest priority, not just the privilege few. America's pastime of sports has clearly taken priority over both advancing and maintaining our nations' position in the world order (pleasure before pain). Be careful the disease affecting the poor will be the order of the day for our nation *emotion-pleasure* over *function-advancement*.

As a nation more investment is in knocking out brains in sports than developing brains to advance our country. The number of Black male athletes paid millions of dollars for our country's pastime pales compared to the glossed-over millions of black students failed to be educated because they did not fit the mold of today's middle-class education model— an utter disgrace, and shame on Uncle Sam.

One may argue education is a local matter, not a national responsibility. But the educational system is a national tragedy and students were better prepared in one room school houses than they are today. My father only completed the 5th grade. However, he supported his family as a tailor, and sent his two daughters to college with no financial aid.

The 2001 No Child Left Behind Act giving States autonomy to create standards of education has failed miserably. School systems are no longer teaching grammar and cursive writing, the mainstays of communication. People cannot speak English without understanding the rules of the language. Future citizens won't be able to sign their signatures if they never learned cursive.

Again, I state, the above descriptions on student-centered strategies are what I am suggesting for improving the educational system.

7

Maslow's Third Level Of Needs

Maslow suggests the third level need is to be loved and to belong. Third level needs are about having interpersonal relationships and being accepted by either large or small groups. Examples of large groups include: religious organizations; social clubs; fraternities; and co-workers. Small groups include family members, intimate partners, close friends, confidants, etc. The needs are to love and to be loved, either sexually or non-sexually.

In low-income communities, this level of need is perhaps the most depleted and misunderstood of all needs described by Maslow. Un-partnered and uncommitted relationships are, unfortunately, characteristic in low-income communities. These feelings of unacceptability can certainly lead to poorly developed self- esteem and depression in the face of poorly evolved genuine love. Going back to the reference made by Dr. Orlando Patterson, "African-Americans have been found to be the most un-partnered people in the Nation." Women, who are wired to be more emotional than male counter-parts, are the first to become emotionally attached when sex is involved. The men, all too often, see sex mostly as a "physical thing."

Sex does not equate to love. Unless these women have experienced family love without strings, especially from males like brothers, fathers, uncles, and grandfathers, they are vulnerable to misinterpretation of attention and physical relationship as love. Further in a female's quest for sustaining a relationship with her partner, she submits to having his baby, believing the myth: if she has his baby, she will have a continuing relationship with him. A continuous relationship with a temporary sex partner is a rare occurrence. The fact is, some of these men tell the woman he wants her to have his baby with no intention of supporting the child either financially or with his presence. He simply wants to prove his virility, which, after all, is the only role Uncle Sam has left him. Uncle Sam promised to take care of his women and children, only if he was not present.

The outside world sees such women as being loose and without morals. Some accuse the women of wanting to have more babies for more welfare money. Maslow suggests these women, like all humans, are searching for love. A woman searches in the nearest place available — her own community with men who don't know how to love unselfishly. These men have had no models, the same situation as the orphaned elephants at the South Africa's Pilanesberg Wildlife Reserve suffered.

Families living in poverty have weak cohesive ties. Marriages and male committed relationships, those living in the home are in a constant state of flux. One cannot count on permanent membership. Often different male partners are coming and going. Often no family name pulls the group together. Names of children are different from the mother's name as she names each child after the "Baby Daddy." There may be two or more Baby Daddies to one female, so the children are half-siblings. The general sense of unity a child needs for self-identity as a family member is missing.

"Relationship terms" signifying connection between members of the family tend to be infrequently used. Rather than acknowledging that a female child is the mother's daughter, the reference is made that she is "my kid." Thus, the child has failed to be defined in a specific relationship as a family member. All children are "kids" in a family. They however, need to know their special position such as a son or daughter. This gives them security of having a special role or position as a family member. Because the ties are so loose and rarely referenced, members of the family are unaware they are a group.

While working at the Department of Social Services as an Administrator within the Department of Juvenile Services under a special grant, we assisted families whose children had committed multiple juvenile offensives. The program was called Family First. One of the many strategies we implemented was to build cohesiveness within the family surrounding the juvenile delinquent.

To do this, the goal was to get loosely connected groups of people to feel like close-knit families. The family of the youth offender was required to hold family meetings at least twice monthly. Each member was given an opportunity to contribute solutions to the youth's challenge. A social worker would initially facilitate the meeting. Gradually, responsibility was turned over entirely to the family.

Next, the family would have to sit down and have dinner together at least twice a week. Most often this was a challenge as the family had no table on which to eat. The family was also required to have a fun night together once a month. This may be an activity such as playing a game, going bowling or going to the movies together. Lastly, the families were encouraged to speak family language, to use terms of endearment and call members by their relationship names such as son, daughter, nephew, cousins, aunt etc.

With these cohesiveness-building activities, the families changed. Staff took pictures of families at the beginning of the program and again after six months of-program participation. The first picture was telling, relative to family members' disconnection. Certain children stood apart from their siblings or mother and appeared disconnected. When the second picture was taken, an amazing change appeared in the photographs. Family members were actually touching and standing close to one another, appearing like a connected family.

One thing different about this program from traditional programs at the department: biological fathers were pursued to participate in resolving issues with their delinquent children. In many cases, the biological fathers participated with better attendance in the parenting groups than court-ordered mothers. Biological fathers confessed they had never been asked to participate in parenting sessions before this invitation was extended. In some instances, the current-boy-friends of the biological mother as well as biological dads participated in the same parenting group.

The parenting groups helped improve family cohesion, meeting the need to belong. Not feeling connected at home is a sure invitation to youth to join a gang to fulfill the need to belong. Gangs emphasize a need for cohesiveness and loyalty. Gangs use special membership colors, signs and other paraphernalia to identify members and have rules and regulations to follow in order to maintain the membership privilege. Certain amount of safety comes with being in a gang, knowing members have each other's back, assurances not felt within loosely connected biological families. The problem with gang membership is the lawless requirements associated with maintaining membership.

The need for a sense of belonging, group identity, as Maslow suggest, is a common characteristic of all human beings at all economic levels. Perhaps not as life altering as gang membership, but nevertheless, holding high priority in many instances. Country Club memberships, Gentlemen Clubs, Sororities, Fraternities, Church membership, Golf Club memberships, Board memberships, and Book Clubs membership, for example, give all members a sense of identity and privilege. Human beings are more alike than different. Differences in functioning comes with the need to make adjustments to different circumstances.

Achievement Acknowledgement

Reaching each Maslow need level is contingent on meeting the previous need level, and broken welfare families meeting any of the dominant needs. Individuals in broken families fail to gain self-esteem or a sense of accomplishment.

Maslow's fourth level is the need for appreciation and respect. One not only has need to accomplish achievement but also need for recognition of personal worth.

Despite the dysfunctions, many Black men and women have reached amazing accomplishments as musicians, poets, athletes, scientist, inventors, educators, and entertainers. Yet acknowledgement of such achievements are all too often slow to be given.

In many instances, Blacks have been under compensated, unrewarded, robbed of recognition or not acknowledged at all.

Such lack of acknowledgment was exposed in the book *Hidden Figures* by Margot Lee Shetterly, later made into a movie. The book exposed the remarkable achievement of Black women working as human computers at NASA, making it possible to launch men into space.

Quality of life in the poverty stricken communities lack order and structure. While the constitution guarantees every American equal rights to life, liberty and the pursuit of happiness, life without purposeful design renders aimless people who lead emotional and unaccomplished lives. Disenchantment and lack of appreciation and respect causes anger and depression which more often leads to violence.

Lack of appreciation and respect resonates with men, in particular, who resort to searching for these attributes. In the neighborhood, personal and street "respect" takes on especially high regard.

To keep from feeling like "a nobody," without appreciation and respect, males in the hood seek this respect from their peers and from the women with whom they have a relationship in negative ways: with symbols of physical power they perceive would solicit such respect. The men display attributes which create fear, producing guns and vicious dogs. They do this to create an illusion of power saying "Don't mess with me," "I have power," and "You must respect me for it."

In their living arrangements, physical violence against women and children reins as an element of demanding respect. Domestic violence and street violence takes on new meaning when couched in one of the Maslow levels the need to be appreciated and respected as a necessary human need. However, the way to achieve respect and appreciation has taken on a negative perspective.

Character qualities calling for respect and appreciation has become illusive due to failure to achieve earlier milestones spelled out in Maslow's Hierarchy of Needs.

Violence can be seriously diminished with a carefully crafted strategic plan to restore families to God's intended design with the natural order of all human needs met.

A sense of achievement can extend to being proud of your home and neighborhood. I once heard a Minister say in a sermon, "You keep praying for a new house but maybe the reason the Lord has not given you one, is because you don't take care of what you already have." He went on to say, "Your current place is unkempt, and your car is trashy like you live out of it and you are comfortable with the way it is ..."

I could see so much truth in his statement. Caring for what you already have, takes motivation. Even a fresh coat of paint can do wonders.

I ran into a young man who had several children by different women but he told me he really wanted to be married but was afraid he would fail at it. He begged me to let him know when I started classes on marriage skills. He met the first criteria for change. He was *motivated.*

As these men are being readied to be head of their families and homes, they must be prepared and motivated to take care of their own property for the sake of their families and neighborhoods. In the majority of the cases, these men have never owned or leased a home or an apartment of their own and they were not encouraged to participate in caring for their mother's home.

Therefore, I am recommending initial programs for restoration of male family leadership start as a residential program. The first step toward leadership is self-sufficiency. As a part of a revived purpose driven life, these men have to learn to stand on their own two feet. Such a residential program would serve as a bridge to self-sufficiency.

The targeted men in need of restoration, having been accustomed to living in someone else's home, must learn to be self-sufficient, and seek to lease or own personal property. Understanding this need, these new candidates of family leaders, must first live independently, learning to take of their own property with a sense of personal achievement. Any restoration leadership program for marriage promotion for men must start with skill sets building independent living. The men must be prepared to be the provider of a home for his new wife and family. When men work to fully sustain themselves, they are more likely and capable of avoiding poverty for themselves and their families.

According to the Census Bureau, the poverty rate in 2013 for married couples with families was about six percent, compared with 30 percent for families with a female head of household and no husband present. During the same period, a *New York Times* article reported children born to married couples were more likely to finish college, find good jobs and have successful marriages.

The deprivation of a balanced socialization left people with an imbalanced emotional orientation response to life. Through a nurturing environment, individuals can be reoriented to a functional life with emotional intelligence. With training participants can be taught to not to be victims of emotional hijacking, and instead taught to be functional: delaying gratification, considering consequences ahead of action, improving goal-setting ability, achieving self-sufficiency and enhancing spiritual identification.

8

The American Dream Deferred

A Dream Deferred by Adverse Conditions not Conducive to Building Male Household Leadership.

Maslow's final and highest level of human needs is "Self-Actualization." It is after having all other needs met, having the ability to reach one's fullest potential. While all may never reach their fullest potential, there is at least the capability or a competitive chance of reaching it. As long as a human has life there is a potential for growth.

When human beings have full access to all that is necessary to reach one's fullest potential, they at least have favorable or running chance at reaching their dream. Dreams and happiness are defined differently by different peoples. However, certain common basic human needs are clearly deserved by all.

Americans take great pride as we reference the history of this great country built on Judeo-Christian tenants and the moral fibers of the founding fathers. With this foundation and under the Spirt of God, these were men who drafted the legal structure and provided a framework and leadership for this nation and its culture. One of the fundamental cultural values this foundation has coveted is men as the heads of household. However, this value has not been afforded to "ALL MEN."

Beyond the years of the Emancipation Proclamation, The Civil Rights Act, and the Voting Rights Act, Black Americans are still fighting for the entitlements guaranteed by the Constitution and Bill of Rights of America as citizens of these United States of America.

In the face of God, *We the People,* who inscribe "In God We Trust" on our money, have drifted from the sentiment of those words.

We the People who fight for freedom around the world for others, shamefully deny its own citizens those conditions of freedom vital to the pursuit of happiness as guaranteed in the Bill of Rights.

We the People have obstructed conditions under which children living in poverty could have a healthy family life but instead, *"We the People"* force their families to choose between financial assistance and a marriage … forcing women to be head of household.

We the People have given newly arrived naturalized citizens more economic support and assistance than Black men and women who also deserve the American Dream and have fought in the Armed Forces to safeguard freedom around the world. For millions of Black Americans the dream has been deferred and deferred and deferred.

We the People have fertilized the soil for "home grown" criminals by first removing the Black male as breadwinner who would be the keeper of the moral family compass, and then blaming the victim by arresting them at higher rates and imprisoning them for longer periods causing basis human needs to go unmet.

The privilege of marriage is a fundamental right of freedom. In recent political battles relative to same sex marriage, constitutional civil law came into question. The final ruling was to legalize same-sex marriage based on guaranteed Constitutional rights of "Life , Liberty and the Pursuit of Happiness.

The Constitutional rights of impoverished Black Americans to the "pursuit of happiness" should be equally guaranteed. While the pursuit of marriage or courtship has continued to be the basis of service discrimination in practice, Uncle Sam continues to blame the victim for dysfunctional living. Should a state of poverty be the basis for denial of Constitutional guarantees?

The First Sin

When God created Adam and then Eve, he had a divine plan. God gave them to each other. He instructed Adam to be the head and Eve to be his helpmate. The two of them were of equal value in His sight but had been given different roles with each depending on the other to work effectively.

In the same way our body has different parts but different roles and each part depend on the other part to do its job effectively. In the body, God created the brain to be the head of the body as He created Adam to be the head of the Family. As we know with the body, if something happens to the head or the brain, other parts will not function properly. If the brain does not give the signal of instructions, to body parts, the parts will be unable to properly perform its task or role. This divine arrangement cannot be changed nor modified and work effectively as it was designed to be.

The Scripture of Adam and Eve in the Garden of Eden reveals God had given Adam very clear instruction regarding the tree from which he was forbidden to eat. He did not give the instruction to Eve but to Adam the head. Adam had been entrusted to keep God's word and lead his family to also follow God's word. What happened instead, Eve became the leader, convincing Adam under the influence of the evil snake to partake of forbidden fruit. Adam failed to hold his position as head as instructed by God. His job as the head was to enforce the instruction of God with his wife. Adam failed his first test. This was the first sin before he ate the fruit followed by many more examples of sin and ultimately leading to destruction of the world.

With the creation of a new world after the flood, God gave an opportunity for new beginnings. God's word never changes. His world order is the same today, as yesterday and tomorrow. HIS word does not change with contemporary thinking and trends. The brain still leads the body and there is still a need to have a leader in every group and the husband is still designated under God as the head of the family.

Black Americans, remove the scales from your eyes and see a new vision. "Write your vision and make it plain." The time has arrived to put away the song "We Shall Overcome." Black Americans have all it takes to do more than "overcome." Blacks can and must "lead." Black men be head of your family as the scripture directs, to start. Then be positive leaders in the communities where you live; be the leader on your job; be in position to write laws and see they are enforced; make the power of your vote change things; and be at the top of this country's economic structure. Let your energy work for you.

Work smart. Stay focused. Change angry energy into productive energy. Live with purpose, giving your energy direction and meaning.

When men lead the neighborhood will change, when the neighbor changes, the community will change, when the community changes, the city will change, when the city changes, the state will changes, when the states changes, the nation will change.

Unless Black people change their plight, they will continue to go round and round in circles, singing a song without a melody, singing it to themselves. Reclaim your self-determination. Reclaim your rhythm of life.

Now it is time for Black men to put guns down and pick up the real amour of your Devine purpose for which you have been created by your Father who is in heaven: Reclaim the position as leader. Protect and subdue the earth for God's Glory.

Men are the caretakers, not the destroyers, of earth and all living creatures … especially human beings. Men are the head, not the tail, and must lead with self-determination rather than be controlled by outside entities, like governmental entitlements, pulling their strings like a puppets.

Men do not need artificial groups, like gangs, to feel safe or important, but can nurture their own home-grown family groups with hope, pride and self-fulfillment.

The male shall accept his role to lead, not boss, his family, and lead with love, temperance and accountability under the scriptural mandates of "Our Father."

Black Americans, "wake up" and move from angry, reactive energy of violence, demonstrations, luting and burning, to using proactive energy by combining resourcefulness, initiative, talents, time, tenacity, and ingenuity to take back what is guaranteed by the Constitution of the United States … the *right* to pursue your happiness without limitations.

No longer wait for some entity to open doors of opportunities for Blacks. Blacks must open their own doors and walk through.

Borrowing from a theme of a recent Family Reunion, I attended in Wilmington NC: Black American men and women, *"Rise Up."*

Take charge of your own destiny.

Move from personal, selfish motives to building up as a "people." And as a people, be empowered to change the trajectory of your peoples' lives.

Earlier Black American Cilvil Rights Leaders such as Martin Luther King, Medgar Evans, Stokley Camichael, Jessie Jackson, Whitney Young, Ralph Abernathy, James Farmer and James Baldwin, to name a few, have already laid ground work, broken down barriers and discrimination laws.

The battle is not over, but change the weapons.

Black men in order to arm yourself with God's Devine purpose, you must have a *blue print* to build a new life, study, understand and follow God's word. Be committed students of His of the scripture as your living manual.

Men go find your children and ask them to forgive you for not being there. Ask your children's mother to forgive you for not being there and thank them for doing the best they could without you.

Thank your children's extended family for standing in the gap when you were not there to carry your part of the load.

Progress does not always call for money. Start with your presence, physical assistance and support.

Work to be committed to one women as your wife, based on the scripture's description of the relationship.

Rear your children according to the Word. The scripture is the book of instruction. Parents have the responsibility to give instructions to their children. Fathers specifically cannot do this if they are not present, nor if their hearts are not committed to the job. The instruction for this is found in Malachi 4:6: "And he shall turn the heart of the fathers to the children, and the heart of the children to their fathers, lest I come and smite the earth with a curse."

Be prepared to financially support your family, working for a noble cause rather than for self-serving motives such as buying the latest pair of tennis shoes. #1 Corinthians 13:11 reminds the changed person: "When I was a child, I spoke as a child, I understood as a child, I thought as a child; but when I became a man, I put away childish things." Mature men take on adult responsibilities.

Because so many babies were not conceived out of love relationships but simply out of physical relationships, these are arduous tasks. Reconciliation of this nature will likely call for added support such as mediators, counselors or reconciliation specialist.

Wholesale reunification of families is uncharted territory. To accomplish these tasks, supportive services must be created and put into place. Enterprising opportunities are plentiful for Black Americans to provide these needed services: to facilitate the reunification and reclaiming process of fathers and children, a Reclamation Bureau can be established. This Bureau would facilitate DNA registrations of children and/or fathers wishing to find or verify paternity for the purpose of reunification. To facilitate a smoother process mediation counselors may be available to neutralize the unification. Unification and reclamation legislation will have to be created and passed to honor and protect the integrity of this movement. Amnesty for past obligation may also be a consideration.

Black Americans must believe and accept the merits to "paternal family orientation." They must believe such a pyridine shift is worth the work. The community as a whole must support this change. God has said on this note, "Go get my sons (and set them free); then go get my daughter (and set them free.)"

Take the lessons from the orphaned Elephants ... disruptions in the natural order of a species will cause chaos and violence. However, change never comes too late.

Jesus answered them, "Truly, truly, I say to you, everyone who practices sin is a slave to sin. The slave does not remain in the house forever; the son remains forever. So if the Son sets you free, you will be free indeed.

John 8:34-35

9

Final Word

My life's work or "calling" started when I was only a child. Our family's movie night was every Wednesday night. My father would take my sister, my mother and I to one of the few black movie theaters in town. There was no checking the papers to see what time the movie started because times were not posted. Folks would arrive at any time and stay until the movie started over again and leave at the point where you had arrived. I was born in 1944 right after World War II had ended in the segregated town of Richmond VA. With a 5th grade education, my father took care of his family as a superb tailor in one of Richmond's prominent men's clothing stores, Newman's, in downtown Richmond.

The thing that sticks out for me in our movie going was stories about children who had been adopted. I was fascinated with those type movies and knew I wanted to own an Orphanage Home and wanted to be a "mother of 100 children." Of course, I had no clue about what it would take to be a mother of 100 children. Yet, this is what I would proudly say when asked " What do you want to do when you grow up?" At the age of 12, my mother firmly scolded me and said I was too old to be going around telling people that I wanted to be a mother of 100 children. Though I didn't quite understand why not, I obeyed her, but never lost my desire to work with adoptions.

I married a preacher two weeks after graduating from Virginia Union University in 1966 and continued my education along with him at Howard University in Washington DC; He in the school of Theology and I in the

School of Social Work.

These were tumultuous times. The Civil Rights Movement was rampant. Folks like Stokely Carmichael, Angela Davis and the likes would show up in our classes at any time. Dr Martin Luther King was assassinated in my graduation year on April 4, 1968. For some reason Howard University became the mecca and central rallying point for the violent reaction to his murder. The campus was filled to capacity with demonstrations that resulted in rioting and burnings in extended areas adjacent to the campus and other areas of the city. A state of emergency resulted in Army trucks and troops lining the streets to enforce with curfews at night fall.

On campus at one point I found myself in a heated debated with a school mate while being unaware that we had been totally surrounded by on-lookers, until I felt my husband's stern hand pulling me out of the crowd that had encircled us. Fact is, he later had to identify me among numerous pictures that were taken by the FBI during the incident. No fear, there were no consequences.

We moved back to Richmond upon my husband's graduation in 1969, as he was called back to our undergraduate Alma Mater, Virginia Union University to become the Dean of Students at the age of 24. Our first child born that same year.

In the early part 1970's, I started my first employment experience in Richmond with the Richmond Department of Social Services in, you may guess , the Adoption Unit. In those days, adoption was pretty much a white institution. I was appalled to find two sets index cards in my office desk drawer of children available for adoption. One small stack, maybe ten white cards representing white babies waiting to be adopted, and a huge stack (maybe 50 +) of orange cards, representing black children waiting to be adopted ranging in age from infancy to eighteen years of age. Obviously, white babies were readily being adopted, while black children were growing up in Foster Care without being adopted; coming into foster care system as infants and leaving the system at the age of 18 years old.

I immediately went on the war path to find permanent homes for these black kids. On my own, I took pictures of these children, made picture albums and went around to churches showing these kids who could be adopted right away. In less than 2 years, I was pushed to become supervisor of a second adoption unit. I say pushed because I was reluctant to leave the "boots on the ground" in the field. In that position as supervisor, however, I approached two local private adoption agencies, Friends Association for Children, a Black adoption agency at that time and The Children's Home Society, a White adoption agency to join me, representing the City, in a collaborative to promote black adoptions. The collaborative was called "Black Home for Black Children." We set up a centralized intake system for those families wanting to adopt by rotating the intake entry point among the three participating agencies. We solicited professional photographers to take free photos of all the waiting children. Through an advertising campaign, we successfully brought attention to the public and other political entities about the need for permanent homes for Black children. Adoption by Black families increased substantially.

Atlas, the Virginia State Department of Social Services woke up, and for the first time acknowledged that Black children were languishing in foster care without being adopted even though they were legally free to be adopted. (I think our efforts had a little something to do with it.) I was invited to serve on a state-wide committee for the Virginia Department of Social Services to address this issue statewide. The Chair of the Committee, Barbara Cotton, a State employee brought to our attention a program started in Chicago by a Catholic Priest whose name is Father George Clements. (a movie was made of his story). The program was called "One Church One Child." Chicago started with a waiting list of over 800 Black kids needing to be adopted. This recruitment program whittled down this list to less than 100 children waiting to be adopted. Chicago received a grant to replicate this program in other States. The committee agreed to look into it for Virginia. The idea of the program is to get "one" church to recruit out of its congregation one family to adopt "one" child. This was a statewide recruitment effort.

Since my Husband is a pastor and I had connections with our state's Baptist General Convention, I volunteered to spear head this effort in

Virginia. To make a long story short, I spearheaded the beginning of this program in 1985, from creating a Board of Director across the State of Virginia to organizing the first five Statewide Conferences, where Churches and local adoption agencies were trained together to resolved this "waiting" problem for black children in Virginia. The Virginia One Church One Child after 30 year, still exists as a supportive and training entity for all the thousands of adoptive families across the State of Virginia.

One could say that I pioneered Black adoptions in Richmond VA. I was featured in Richmond Magazine as well as a full page article in the Richmond Times Dispatch. My husband and two other original founding board members are still on the Board. My husband is both the president of the Virginia OCOC Board of Directors as well as president of the National Board of Directors of One Church One Child.

In the early '90's I became the Program Administrator for all of the Child Welfare Programs for the City of Richmond which included Adoption, Foster Care and Child Protective Services (CPS). There were over 900 children in Foster Care at that time. Finally, I was a "mother of over 100" orphaned children. It was my job to see that life altering decisions were made in the best interest of these children through my staff. After having three biological children, my husband and I also adopted our fourth child.

For 10 years 1996–2006, I worked in the heart of the East End of with five Housing Development entities predominantly black low income mothers and children.

I created an innovative program thru the City Manager's Office within the Richmond Department of Juvenile Justice Services called " Family First." The goal of the program was to restore parental authority (both mothers and fathers) back to parents who lost control of their youth. For the first time in the history of the Department of Social Services, fathers were sort and included in the family restoration process. This program drew attention of the then governor of Virginia, Governor George Allen who invited us to showcase our work at his Statewide Conference.

I have lectured at the University of Richmond, Virginia Commonwealth University and Norfolk State University on concepts presented in the pending publication For years colleagues have urged me to publish this information. In addition to this work I was the Administrator over a program called Healthy Families, a National Accredited home visitation program focusing on the prevention of child abuse and neglect.

Recently I was in the company of several workers from the Virginia Department of Social Services. They mention that one of the best programs that they could remember came from Richmond City called "Family First." Needless to say I was happy to claim its creation.

After retiring in 2006, I worked for a program for almost seven years called "Boaz and Ruth." It was a faith based program designed to support men and women transitioning from prison life to society. The program itself was located in the Highland Park Community, *"smack dab"* in the middle of "the hood." In this work, I came full circle to again to working with "orphans," but this time, it was with adult "orphans" mostly living on the streets "the hood" without the benefit, direction and support of mature leadership. The clients were predominantly male and predominantly African American. The program format called for life preparation classes in the morning and on-the-job-training for the balance of the day in one of several social enterprises. These enterprises were namely a restaurant, a second hand furniture store, a moving company, a furniture restoration shop, all in preparation to become economically independent

In my position, I taught restoration classes to all participants including women but mostly African American men. I designed a curriculum which addressed subjects from "Healing and Forgiveness of Their Families of Origin" to "Male /Female Relationships" and "How to Picking the Right Partner." This hands-on experience pulled on all of my life work's and experience in one setting. It was an epiphany from the Creator that these experiences along with my education, other employment and volunteer work had prepared me for this work of restoring of the low income Black families. I underwent a spiritual renewal and transformation myself. All of my life's work was for *His purpose.*

I am not just telling this story for the first time. Back in the 90's I remember the first time I told this story to a group of men from "the hood." Their responses were amazing! They were so relieved to learn that their circumstances were not their fault. They began slapping each other's hands and asking me "Why they don't tell this stuff in church?" It surprised me that they immediately connected this to Church when I never mentioned anything spiritual. They even said, let's not tell the women yet. (In that moment they apparently forgot that I was a woman.) And now God directed me, "Go get my sons first and then get my daughters."

I was recently recognized in a book authored by Jim Doherty entitled *Finishing Up Strong* featuring vignettes of accomplished and prominent men and women over the age of 70 who have made significant contribution to society in the Richmond Community. The featured article on me spoke of my recent work in the area of black men.

Over the years my volunteer work included:

President of the Board of Directors of the Richmond YWCA (It was under my tenure that we started the Annual Outstanding Women of the Year Awards)

Member of Board of Directors Hope in the Cities (Initiative of Change—giving direction and oversight to a program designed to bring about Racial Reconciliation in the Richmond Community. Associated with its goal, I became a trained Facilitator of group dialogs and a trained Workshop Facilitator.)

President of Board of Director of Martin Luther King Counseling Center

Vice Chair of the Trustee Board of Fifth Baptist Church

Member of Board of Director of First Things First (which gave oversight to their program which promoted healthy marriages thru education and training. I became certified in many marriage relationship tools.)

The focus of this book is to stop the *violence in our communities* by restoring the integrity of intact married families among low income African Americans and thereby giving children the benefits of both gender resources in their development. My target audience are those entities or sphere of influences that impact family formation such as government policy makers, educators and professional who design service models and curriculum for schools of social work and spiritual leaders. The book also targets practitioners of constitutional law who may seek legal remedy on behalf of the black men who have been denied conditions vital to their pursuit of happiness. Lastly, this book is to educate the general public on the impact of misguided legislation and the profound negative effect it has had on generations of children and adults.

Relevant reading from Bold Venture

A Date With the Executioner
by Ellen Smith

This non-fiction true crime story is a must-read now that Social Justice Reform is a prominent topic in our national dialogue. A woman's memoir of a charismatic brother, processed by the penal system and sent to death. The author relates her tormented mother's futile attempts to find help for her brother — before he was executed by the system that ignored him.

The Taxol Thief
by Ceylon Barclay

For three decades, the FDA denied approval of a first-in-class drug, "taxol," condemning thousands of breast-cancer victims to certain death. *The Taxol Thief* is the story a couple's fight for life — by smuggling taxol from China through Russia. So begins Troy Locke's odyssey, a journey fraught with political chicanery and wrongful imprisonment.

Guide to American Culture
by William P. Lazarus, M.A.

A road map to an American culture for new and old citizens alike. For Americans, it's a reminder how much has changed since Christopher Columbus made landfall in the New World. Topics include: History, Politics, Communication, Education, Law, Race, Religion, American West, War 1700s to 1900s, War 1900s to current, Folk Heroes, Major Sports, Entertainment, Arts, and Daily Life.

www.boldventurepress.com

Relevant reading from Bold Venture

Once a Pulp Man
Audrey Parente

Judson P. Philips, author of *Cancelled in Red*, had two lucrative writing careers. He filled pages in magazines like *Argosy* under his own name, and wrote for slick magazines and paperbacks as Hugh Pentecost. *Once a Pulp Man* unveils the author whose personal life was as complicated as any mystery plot.

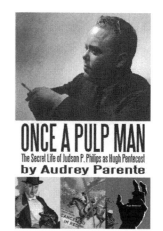

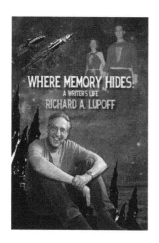

Where Memory Hides
by Richard A. Lupoff

Where Memory Hides is a guided tour through the life and career of mystery and science fiction's most versatile practitioner. A professional author for six decades, and a life-time fan of everything, Lupoff's tome is part autobiography, movie and book reviews, writing class, and tales writing and publishing. Lupoff regales readers with triumphs and tribulations from his six-decade plus career.

Pulp Jazz: The Charles Boeckman Story
by Charles Boeckman

Charles Boeckman's biography often reads like the stuff of pulp fiction. A young jazz musician by night, and author of hard-hitting pulp fiction by day. The recipient a Texas Music Walk of Fame star, he recollects his life, work, and authors and musicians he met along the journey. This edition features three of his short stories — including "Ambition," later adapted to an episode of *Alfred Hitchcock Presents*.

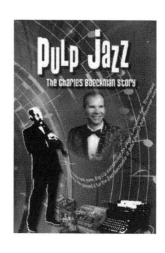

www.boldventurepress.com

Relevant reading from Bold Venture

Sands of Time: 100 Years of Racing
by William P. Lazarus

The Sands of Time takes readers on a wild ride through a century of NASCAR action — from the first makeshift race in 1903 to the incredible panorama of the Daytona 500. Each phase is accented with colorful anecdotes, featuring the early 1900s cultured drivers, to the roughnecks from the Southern woods, to today's athletes who dare the high banks at 200 mph.

Around the Turn
by William P. Lazarus

Race cars careening around yet another turn seem common-place today, but the sport had to maneuver around some daunting roadblocks to get to the start-finish line and faces more in the future. In *Around the Turn*, race historian Bill Lazarus documents NASCAR's greatest triumphs, and some of its more bizarre moments ... *Around the Turn* is a great companion to *Sands of Time: Celebrating 100 Years of Racing*.

Guide to American Culture
by William P. Lazarus, M.A.

A road map to an American culture for new and old citizens alike. For Americans, it's a reminder how much has changed since Christopher Columbus made landfall in the New World. Topics include: History, Politics, Communication, Education, Law, Race, Religion, American West, War 1700s to 1900s, War 1900s to current, Folk Heroes, Major Sports, Entertainment, Arts, and Daily Life.

www.boldventurepress.com

Relevant reading from Bold Venture

Love Story Writer
by Daisy Bacon

Daisy Bacon edited Street & Smith's *Love Story Magazine*, arguably the most successful romance-themed pulp fiction magazine of all time. In her words, Miss Bacon shares her insights and experience in managing a successful publication and authoring romantic fiction. Introductions and afterwords by pop culture historians Laurie Powers and Michelle Nolan.

Timely Confidential
by Allen Bellman

Allen Bellman recalls his life and career in the Golden Age of Comics, working for Marvel Comics before it was known by its famous name; friction between different divisions of artists and writers; brushes with celebrities; a second career as a graphic designer and photographer; a move from the New York region to the Florida tropics; and his return to comic book fandom nearly six decades after leaving the field.

The Plot Genie Index
by Wycliffe A. Hill

THIS is the iconic plotting device that inspired Gillian Conoley's novel *The Plot Genie*. You've heard the tall tales — Now it's time to write your own tall tales! The book lists hundreds of locales, characters, dramatic situations, and plot twists. When used in conjunction with the Plot Robot (TM) spinner wheel, the author promised it would generate enough ideas to keep an author busy for years.

www.boldventurepress.com

Continuing series from Bold Venture Press ...

Zorro: The Complete Pulp Adventures

Six volumes by Johnston McCulley

In the early 1800s, California was still under Spanish rule. Some of the military commanders plundered and won riches at the expense of the peace-loving settlers. Against these agents of injustice, the settlers were powerless, until one man arose whose courage inspired Californians and gave them the spirit to resist tyranny. *That man was Zorro!*

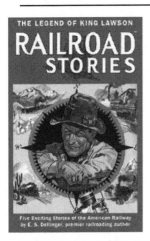

Railroad Stories

Adventure on the American railways!

All aboard for romance, danger, and plain old American hard work! Classic pulp fiction tales of the railways! For decades, readers were entertained each month with *Railroad Stories Magazine* and it's blend of factual articles and fiction yarns. This is wholesome he-man fiction for railroad fans, written by authors who knew trains first-hand!

Pulp Adventures

Audrey Parente, editor

Every issue is a voyage across the landscape of pulp fiction — mystery, science fiction, horror, romance, western, and more! from lush jungles to sun-baked deserts, lawless wild west towns to utopian cities of the future! Don your pith helmets and fedoras and embark on great reading!

www.boldventurepress.com

Made in the USA
Columbia, SC
11 May 2019